You Are My Hiding Place, Lord

Emilie Barnes

HARVEST HOUSE PUBLISHERS

EUGENE, OREGON

Unless otherwise indicated, all Scripture quotations are taken from the HOLY BIBLE, NEW INTERNATIONAL VERSION®. NIV®. Copyright © 1973, 1978, 1984 by the International Bible Society. Used by permission of Zondervan. All rights reserved.

Verses marked NLT are taken from the *Holy Bible,* New Living Translation, copyright © 1996, 2004. Used by permission of Tyndale House Publishers, Inc., Wheaton, IL 60189 USA. All rights reserved.

Verses marked NKJV are taken from the New King James Version. Copyright © 1982 by Thomas Nelson, Inc. Used by permission. All rights reserved.

Verses marked TLB are taken from *The Living Bible,* Copyright © 1971. Used by permission of Tyndale House Publishers, Inc., Wheaton, IL 60189 USA. All rights reserved.

Verses marked NASB are taken from the New American Standard Bible®, © 1960, 1962, 1963, 1968, 1971, 1972, 1973, 1975, 1977, 1995 by The Lockman Foundation. Used by permission. (www.Lockman.org)

Verses marked AMP are taken from The Amplified Bible, Copyright © 1954, 1958, 1962, 1964, 1965, 1987 by The Lockman Foundation. All rights reserved. Used by permission. (www.Lockman.org)

Select devotional material adapted from *Minute Meditations for Busy Moms* by Emilie Barnes, Copyright © 2002.

Cover by Dugan Design Group, Bloomington, Minnesota

Cover photo © Corbis Photography / Veer

YOU ARE MY HIDING PLACE, LORD
Copyright © 2009 by Emilie Barnes
Published by Harvest House Publishers
Eugene, Oregon 97402
www.harvesthousepublishers.com

Library of Congress Cataloging-in-Publication Data

Barnes, Emilie.
You are my hiding place, Lord / Emilie Barnes.
  p. cm.
ISBN 978-0-7369-2670-6 (pbk.)
1. Christian women—Prayers and devotions. I. Title.
BV4844.B363 2009
242'.643—dc22

                                                          2008049425

Printed in the United States of America

09 10 11 12 13 14 15 16 17 / DP-NI / 10 9 8 7 6 5 4 3 2 1

This book is dedicated to the founder of Harvest House Publishers, Mr. Bob Hawkins, Sr. Without his faith in me over 25 years ago, I would not have been able to write 70 books. He saw something in me that I wasn't able to see in myself. He took a gamble to publish my first book, *More Hours in My Day*.

His vision gave me the encouragement to be all that he saw in me.

I am forever grateful and thankful for him and for all the encouragement he has given to me over these many years.

—*Emilie Barnes*

Introduction

Thou art my hiding place; thou shalt preserve
me from trouble; thou shalt compass me about
with songs of deliverance.

PSALM 32:7 KJV

My experiences in life have confirmed to me that God is truly my hiding place. He is closer than a brother. One to whom I can go to in all phases of life. I have written these pages so you might be encouraged in your journey through life as David did in his life. I have lived out each of the following thoughts about life. As you read them, I will be encouraged if they help you along your life's path.

A unique feature of this book is that you don't have to start at the beginning. You can skip around and choose the reading that seems most suited for the day ahead. At the top of each page you will see three boxes ☐ ☐ ☐. Each time you read one of these offerings, put a checkmark in one of the boxes. In this way you can keep track of those selections you have read.

There is a prayer given after every selection. It is there to give you a kernel of thought. Hopefully, you will be able to give your own prayer.

Each meditation closes with a recommended "action" that can

help you implement or reinforce what you need for your daily life. I encourage you to keep a journal while you go through this devotional so that you can record your thoughts, prayers, and praises during your quiet time. Whatever you are going through, this journal will become a reminder of how God cares for you in your time of need. His faithfulness will shine through.

May this book be an encouragement for you during your difficult circumstances and those days that are filled with stress or worry. The journey is made richer and lighter when you live it in God's wisdom and love.

> My most cherished possession I wish I could leave you is my faith in Jesus Christ, for with Him and nothing else you can be happy, but without Him and with all else you'll never be happy.
>
> —Patrick Henry

You Are My Hiding Place

I love Your law.
You are my hiding place and my shield.
Psalm 119:113-114 NKJV

As a little girl, I loved to play hide-and-seek. After the sun had gone down and it started to get dark, I delighted to find a secret place where no one could find me. When I stayed there, I felt so secure knowing that no one was going to catch me. As I grew older, I kept looking for such a place where I could get away from all the pressures of life.

When I became a Christian and started to have a daily quiet time with my Lord, I was soon aware that my "prayer closet" had become my new hiding place. This was a place where I felt safe from the world, and I could take all the time I needed to read God's Word. My "prayer closet" is an actual place in my home, but I can transport the security of a sanctuary to the beach, to a mountain cabin, or to a desert condo. My place of prayer is actually wherever I meet with God, and you can create the same refuge no matter where you live. Don't confine your quiet time to just one location. God's comfort and love is our hiding place whenever we need it. Do you talk to God throughout the day? If not, how come? Do you think your life isn't important enough or your concerns big enough? Or do you just get so busy that it doesn't occur to you to talk to God while you're in the car, at work, or waiting for the kids to get out of school? Don't miss out on the wonders of communication with God. Being able to run to His embrace in every moment is one of the many gifts we receive as believers. He is right here for you.

When the stress of the day is getting to you, think of the safety you feel in your hiding place. Knowing God is always with you will calm your spirit.

Prayer: Father God, I look so forward to meeting You each day at an appointed time. Your Scriptures still my soul. My anxieties are washed away after our times together. Thank You! Amen.

Action: Turn to God in prayer today. Consider how you feel when you place your life and your cares in the sanctuary of God's heart and love. This is your hiding place forever.

Faith Is a Gift

Now faith is the assurance of things hoped for,
the conviction of things not seen.

HEBREWS 11:1 NASB

Do you have trouble believing in something you haven't seen? The disciple Thomas did. He couldn't bring himself to believe in Jesus' resurrection until he actually saw and touched Jesus.

Jesus told Thomas, "Because you have seen me, you have believed; blessed are those who have not seen and yet have believed" (John 20:29). I don't believe Jesus was scolding Thomas when He said these words. He was just saying that Thomas would be a lot happier—that's what "blessed" means!—if he could learn to take some things on faith!

I think that's true for many of us. We have faith, and yet we keep asking for proof or more clarification. God doesn't reprimand us because of this. He lovingly reveals Himself time after time. However, we are missing out on the abundance of a life lived out in absolute faith when we question more than we rest in God's peace!

What is so incredible is that every day I take it on faith that my car will start, my TV will click on, my internet server will function. All of these seem like miracles to me! But they work—at least most of the time! So if I can manage to believe in these man-made miracles, why should I have trouble believing in God and His divine miracles? Though I haven't physically seen Him, I have felt His presence. I have seen His works. As a result, I no longer waste my energy fussing over whether God is real. Instead, I choose to enjoy the blessing of belief.

Prayer: Father God, I'm so thankful that I have not let the world blind my eyes to You. You are there even with all the smoke screens of life. I know You are there even though I can't see You. Amen.

Action: In what area of your life do you not have faith? Give all of your life to God's care, including this area or these areas. Thank God for the many miracles and promises that He has revealed to you in your life.

Give Prayer a Try

Because he bends down and listens,
I will pray as long as I breathe!
PSALM 116:2 TLB

Who has time to pray? My 'To Do' list is always longer than my day. I run from the time the alarm goes off in the morning until I fall into bed at night. How can I possibly find time to do one more thing? When could I fit in even a few minutes to read the Bible or pray?"

I thought that way for many years, but finally I decided to make prayer one of my top priorities. I started to get up 30 minutes before the rest of the family awakened each day, and I spent that time with God. The days that I did this went so much smoother. I had more control of the day, and my emotional stability was much more even. I'm glad I established this habit in my life; because, now when I face dark times, I already have a line of communication with my heavenly Father. We became prayer partners long ago and what an amazing blessing that has been in my life. You can have this same relationship and connection with God daily.

Are you wondering what to talk to God about when you pray? Here are a few suggestions.

- Praise God for who He is—the Creator and Sustainer of the whole universe, who is interested in each of us (Psalm 150; Matthew 10:30).

- Thank God for what He has done for you, for all He is doing for you, and for all that He will do for you (Philippians 4:6).

- Confess your sins. Tell God about the things you have done and said and thought for which you are sorry. He tells us in 1 John 1:9 that He is "faithful and just to forgive us our sins."

- Pray for your family and for friends or neighbors who have needs—physical and spiritual. Ask God to work in the heart of someone you hope will come to know Jesus as Savior. Pray for your government officials, for your minister, and for missionaries and other Christian servants (Philippians 2:4).

Pray, too, for yourself. Ask for guidance for the day ahead. Ask God to help you do His will, and ask Him to arrange opportunities to serve Him throughout the day.

Prayer: Father God, may I never forget to call on You in every situation. Amen.

Action: Decide today that you will give prayer a try. See what talking to God can do.

The Making of a Home

Unless the LORD builds the house, its builders labor in vain.
PSALM 127:1

Do you sometimes feel that your house has become a place to repair broken objects, mow the lawn, pay off the mortgage, serve quick meals, and put in a few hours of sleep each night?

There was a time when my home felt just like that. But finally I figured out that a real home is much more than all that; it's a place where people live, grow, laugh, cry, learn, and create together.

After watching his house burn down, a small child was quoted as saying, "We still have a home. We just don't have a house to put it in." He understood what a home really was.

Our home should be a grace center for the whole family. We don't have to be perfect—just forgiven. Everywhere else—school, work, neighborhood, church—people expect us to be perfect. Our home is a place where we can be ourselves. We all need a place to be just us, with no pretense. We can laugh when we feel like it and cry when we need to. We can grow, we can make mistakes, we can agree, and we can disagree. Home should be a place where happy experiences occur—a place sheltered from the problems of the world and a place of love, acceptance, security, and faith.

When we read the morning newspaper, we are confronted with all the tragedies around us. We realize the world outside our front door is falling apart, but within our four walls we can offer a place called home.

> The Christian home is the Master's workshop, where the processes of character-molding are silently, lovingly, faithfully, and successfully carried on.
>
> —Richard M. Milnes

What can we do to have a home like God intended? As with everything in life, when something is broken we go back to the instruction manual. In this case, it's the Bible. The home is God's idea—not something invented by twenty-first-century Americans. In the original plan of creation, God designed the home to be the foundation of society—a place to meet the mental, spiritual, physical, and emotional needs of people.

Scripture states that marriage is a permanent relationship not to be divided. Marriage is instituted by God to accomplish His plans in our society. In marriage a husband and wife become "one," building a permanent relationship. It's not a temporary convenience to be maintained as long as it feels good. God designed the family as an enduring relationship in which, with His care, humans could weather the storms of life together. The home is God's loving shelter for growing to maturity.

God is not only the designer, but He also wants to take the headship of family life. He wants to guide and to give love, peace, and forgiveness abundantly. We've got our work cut out for us if we want a true home. We must live life with a big purpose—to have not just a house but a home.

Prayer: Father God, You know I want our house to be more than just a place—I want it to be a home. I want to yield to Your leadership. Give me wisdom, understanding, and knowledge. Amen.

Action: Pray for your home and its various members.

The Spirit of Femininity

The young lady was beautiful of form and face.
ESTHER 2:7 NASB

When I was a little girl, I dreamed of being a "lady." The world of *Little Women* with its gracious manners and old-fashioned, flowing dresses fascinated me. Softness and lace, tantalizing fragrance and exquisite texture, a nurturing spirit, and a love of beauty—these images of femininity shaped my earliest ideas of loveliness.

Is that kind of femininity a lost value today? I don't believe it. The world has changed, and most of us live in simple shirts or business suits or jeans instead of flowing gowns. But I still believe that somewhere in the heart of most of us is a little girl who longs to be a lady.

I also believe that today's world is hungering to be transformed by the spirit of femininity. What better antidote for an impersonal and violent society than warm, gentle, feminine strength? What better cure for urban sprawl and tracked-out countrysides than a love of beauty and a confidence in one's ability to make things lovely? What better hope for the future than a nurturing mother's heart that is more concerned for the next generation than for its own selfish desires? All these qualities—gentle strength, love of beauty, care and nurturing—are part of the spirit of femininity.

Being a woman created by God is such a privilege—and the gift of our femininity is something we can give both to ourselves and to the people around us. Just one flower, one candle, can warm up a cold, no-nonsense atmosphere with an aura of "I can."

Women have always had the ability to transform an environment to make it comfortable and inviting. I believe we should rejoice in that ability and make the most of it.

The spirit of femininity is so many things. To me, it is expressed in objects chosen for their beauty as well as their usefulness and lovingly cared for. It is demonstrated when people are accepted and nurtured, loveliness embraced and shared. Most important about the spirit of femininity is the spirit of care and compassion. In my mind, the most feminine woman is one with an eye and ear for others, and a heart for God.

> Whatever is true, whatever is noble, whatever is right, whatever is pure, whatever is lovely, whatever is admirable—if anything is excellent or praiseworthy—think about such things.
>
> —PHILIPPIANS 4:8

Prayer: Father God, let my heart be opened to those things that reflect the love of God to those who are around me. I want to be a sweet fragrance to the world. Amen.

Action: Evaluate who you are—be willing to change those areas that need to be softened—ask a friend to hold you accountable.

The Strength You Need

He gives strength to the weary,
and to him who lacks might He increases power.
ISAIAH 40:29 NASB

Are you always tired? As a busy mom, I yearned for rest and sleep. The activities of the day often seemed beyond my strength. At no other time in my life can I remember ever being so utterly drained of energy. Each day I looked forward to evening when I could tuck the children into bed and get some well-needed rest.

Looking back, I'm sure those days weren't much fun for my husband, Bob, either. When he came home from work, my energy had long since been sapped by the day's activities. By age 21, I was responsible for five children—our two and my brother's three children whom Bob and I took in. Life at that time absolutely overwhelmed me. Later, after the children were grown, Bob and I were busy with our More Hours in My Day ministries and that too required a great deal of energy and time. It was a gift, just like parenting, because it required me to depend on God's strength every day.

When we have low physical reserves, we are open prey for the enemy. Satan can attack us with all sorts of accusations about our lot in life.

His goal is to cause us to resent the demands made on us and to cast doubt on God's faithfulness.

But God knows our weaknesses and in every case will send the strength we need for every day's circumstances. No more, no less. Just enough.

Don't be discouraged by your weaknesses. God knows your need. He really does. It's human to be tired after a mom's full day, but how we handle our tiredness is of utmost importance. Our power for living must depend on faith in the source of our power—Jesus Christ.

Prayer: Lord, my Strength, when I feel weak, let me rely on Your strength. I will not let Satan take advantage of my tiredness. Instead I turn to You and receive the victory set aside for me in Christ. Amen.

Action: During times of extreme stress, look fully to His great promise that He gives power to the weak and He increases strength to those who have no might. Claim this as your "tired promise." Do it as often as necessary—even if it's every day!

A cord of three strands is not quickly broken.
ECCLESIASTES 4:12

Many times we look to others to help us out, and we complain when we don't receive the help we think we deserve. However, help starts from within ourselves first, then comes from outside.

As a busy mom, I often had to depend upon myself to get something done. Often there was no one around to help during the hectic schedule of a busy day. Perhaps your life is like that too. Take heart—you will get everything done that needs to be done.

At such times, it helps to take an inventory of all the skills and tools God has so graciously given us at birth. We tend to take for granted these attributes for success that were given to us at the very beginning of our lives—our eight fingers and two thumbs.

And although we need to dig in and do our own work, sometimes we do need the help of others. King Solomon in all his wisdom tells us that friends are great blessings to us:

> Two are better than one because they have a good return
> for their labor...But woe to the one who falls when there is
> not another to lift him up...If two lie down together they

keep warm...if one can overpower him who is alone, two can resist him. A cord of three strands is not quickly torn apart (Ecclesiastes 4:9-12 NASB).

Are you working on relationships that build these friendly blessings?

Begin at home with your family members. Throughout Scripture we are reminded to be united, be of the same spirit, be of one accord. Unity should be our goal: wife to husband, parents to children, children to siblings, friend to friend. Your church should be a source of help too. How well do you know the other mothers in your church? Have you reached out to offer help to another mother when she needs it? A good family church is a great place from which to build a network of moms who can help each other through the rough times of motherhood.

Prayer: Lord, let me fully realize the gift of my ten fingers that You have given me. May I also be appreciative of the other friends You have given me. Help me to be available to serve other mothers as I wish to be helped. Amen.

Action: Call a friend or write her a letter. Be sure to tell her how much you appreciate her friendship. Or write a note to your pastor or to a mentor who has influenced your life.

Knowing God in Stillness

Be still, and know that I am God.
PSALM 46:10 NKJV

Our culture is severely overstimulated. Loud music at home, the mall, and even at most restaurants. Advertisements fill everything we read, hear, and see. No wonder we live in an era when people are nervous, have short attention spans, have hearing problems, and have a difficult time being still.

Do we even bother to listen for stillness, quietness, and silence anymore? Do we take moments for reflection and rest so that we can clear our heads and talk to God?

For some people who have become addicted to noise, the "sound" of silence is very uncomfortable. They become uneasy, nervous, twitching; they need sounds—loud sounds. They want to mask the thoughts that rise up or the worries that might surface if they spend time in silence. Try telling teenagers (or most adults) to stop listening to their iPod or to turn off the television, and they get upset, frustrated, and even angry.

Our culture is missing out on something great and important. Quiet times are refreshing to the soul, offering us reflection, perhaps a chance to mourn or to be happy or maybe even to hear God speak to us in a still, small voice.

Do such times exist in your home? Or is your house filled with the discordant sounds of television and pop music? Is it any wonder that many of us and our children do not know how to cultivate silence? Our hearts are longing for such peace, but we cover up that longing with more noise, more activity, and more distractions.

Perhaps your children are already well on the road to the addiction to noise—the need for constant audio activity. If so, you will be shortchanging them by not teaching them the joys of pure silence and the treasure of prayer.

The psalmist knew that in order to know God, we have to stop striving and become still. The business of life must come to a halt in order to know God.

Prayer: God of Peace, I find myself anxious; help me establish a quiet time each day so I can be still. In this stillness let me ponder who You are and may I know You in a greater way. Help me to establish my home as a place of peace, not audio discord. Amen.

Action: When you find yourself with a hectic schedule and aren't sure you can get everything done, that is the moment to call "time-out" and seek the quietness that God can give you. Practice stillness for 90 seconds to restore your sense of direction. It doesn't take long.

Growing Daily in Godliness

If each moment is sacred—a time and place where
we encounter God—life itself is sacred.
JEAN M. BLOOMQUIST

I believe a godly woman is one who possesses inner peace and tranquility; she doesn't have to prove herself to anyone. She is strong and yet she doesn't use her strength to control or dominate people; neither does she depend on recognition from others. Hers is an inner contentment and satisfaction based not on accomplishments, position, or authority, but on a deep awareness of God's eternal and personal love for her.

That kind of inner peace, strength, confidence, and tranquility comes from depending on God, obeying Him, drawing on His strength and wisdom, and learning to be like Him. When this happens in our lives, we gradually grow free of anxious competitiveness and aggressiveness. We have no need to prove our worth and value because we know how much we are worth in God's sight, and then we are free to reach out in love to others.

I've seen that spirit at work in the lives of so many beautiful Christian women—women of all ages and every walk of life. I think of a young lady who was 25 years old when I first met her at the Edmonton airport in Alberta, Canada. In the two days we spent together, I could see the spirit of godliness shining in the life of this young woman. She had a vision for her family and the women of her church to become more Christ-centered, and that vision was contagious.

I also think of a lovely 92-year-old woman who attended one of my organizational seminars. This amazing lady sat through all four sessions, scribbling notes the entire time. I remember thinking, "At 92, who even cares?" But this new friend told me she wanted to learn everything she could in life so she could pass on her learning to younger women. Her teachable spirit humbled and blessed me. I only hope that when I am 92, I will be as eager to learn and to grow in God's grace.

Godly values—spiritual awareness, obedience, trust, self-giving love—are so different from the values that seem to run this worldly age. And yet God's strategy for growth and happiness has been around for more than 2000 years. Countless generations of women who have taken it seriously have found that it works. I pray that we might take it seriously as well, growing daily in godliness and modeling godliness in our homes and lives.

Prayer: Father God, I daily need a reminder what my priorities are in life. Help me be more Christlike in my everyday life. Amen.

Action: Read Galatians 5:22-23. Identify one of these nine attributes of Christ and begin to live out this characteristic in your Christian life.

Surviving the Storm

A righteous man may have many troubles,
but the LORD delivers him from them all.
PSALM 34:19 NIV

In the past few years we have all witnessed—if not experienced—some very traumatic storms and natural disasters. It grieves us all when others face such devastation and we strive to do what we can to help those who have lost homes, loved ones, or hope. With this in mind, it is good for us to remember that not every storm faced is a literal storm. During our lifetime, all of us will experience storms that are as devastating as these tragedies of tornados, floods, hurricanes, fires. They may not be as evident as a hurricane, but when you experience them, they are just as real to you. Such storms can turn our lives around—can turn our dreams into hellish nightmares. These storms are called divorce, disease, death, betrayal, bankruptcy, abuse, adultery—all kinds of addiction.

What do we do when these storms hit our lives? God has us covered. As we pray and seek His guidance, we are to immediately go to Scripture and embrace what God has to say about our circumstance, lives, direction, and needs great and small. Prepare your heart for the storms ahead by becoming familiar with God's Word and its message.

God has a purpose for our lives.

- "We know that God causes all things to work together for good to those who love God, to those who are called according to His purpose" (Romans 8:28 NASB).

- "Everyone who asks receives, and he who seeks finds, and to him who knocks it will be opened" (Matthew 7:8 NASB).

- "All things you ask in prayer, believing, you will receive" (Matthew 21:22).

We have God's presence. In Mark 6:47-48 and John 11:33-35, we read that Jesus was with each person in the storm. He did not leave them alone. In each of our life's storms He is with us.

- "My presence shall go with you, and I will give you rest" (Exodus 33:14 NASB).

- "Be strong and courageous! Do not tremble or be dismayed, for the LORD your God is with you wherever you go" (Joshua 1:9 NASB).

- "I will never desert you, nor will I ever forsake you" (Hebrews 13:5 NASB).

We have the peace of God.

- "In my distress I called upon the LORD, and cried to my God for help; He heard my voice out of His temple, and my cry for help before Him came into His ears" (Psalm 18:6 NASB).

- "Why are you troubled, and why do doubts arise in your hearts?" (Luke 24:38 NASB).

- "Peace I leave with you; My peace I give to you; not as the world gives do I give to you. Do not let your heart be troubled, nor let it be fearful" (John 14:27 NASB).

We have God's power.

- "You will receive power when the Holy Spirit has come upon you" (Acts 1:8 NASB).
- "My grace is sufficient for you, for power is perfected in weakness. Most gladly, therefore, I will rather boast about my weaknesses, that the power of Christ may dwell in me" (2 Corinthians 12:9 NASB).
- "God has not given us a spirit of timidity, but of power and love and discipline" (2 Timothy 1:7 NASB).

How will we respond when the storms occur? Don't look down, don't look back, but look upward toward the heavens and ask God to give you a new vision and purpose for this event. In our family, when the storm crashes in our lives, we ask God this question: "What lesson are you trying to teach us in this experience?"

Don't keep what you learn from your storms to yourself. Be available and willing to help others as they stand against the storms of life. And always seek God's strength to offer that help to your neighbor, loved one, and the stranger in need.

Prayer: Father God, show me Your purpose for each of my storms. Let me learn something—if I don't, those storms will be of no value for my life. From Scripture and experience I know You are always with me. Amen.

Action: Write down in your journal an experience of peace you have had in a storm of your life. Read Paul's prayer in Ephesians 1:18-21.

Keep Your Word

A faithful man [woman] will abound with blessings.
PROVERBS 28:20 NASB

We are repeatedly challenged to understand what it means to be faithful to God. We know we're supposed to be dedicated and committed, but when we see faithfulness wavering in the lives of those around us, it can be difficult to remember what it means to have this virtue. The first thing we must do is look at our actions. When we exhibit the fruit of faithfulness, we show up on time, finish the job, are there when we need to be, and do what we say we are going to do. One of the Barnes' favorite mottoes is: "Just do what you say you are going to do!" Can you imagine what a difference living out this motto would make on the job, with your spouse and children, at church, and in your own life? The results would be amazing!

A successful life is based on trust and faith. Throughout the Old Testament, we read of God's faithfulness to the people of Israel. No matter how much the Israelites complained about their situation, God remained true to His chosen people. In the New Testament, Jesus reflected the same loyalty to His heavenly Father. He always sought God's will. Jesus' faithfulness took Him all the way to the cross so that our sins could be eternally covered.

Do you trust God and have faith in His leading as you journey through your own deserts—your own trials? Do you stand for faith and follow through with what you say you are going to do? Some of us have had people cross our paths who have not kept their word to us, and it has hurt us deeply. That can make it difficult to trust those people around us now and even difficult to trust God. But one of the best ways to overcome the fear of relying on God's strength is to become a strong and faithful servant. You will discover that as you keep your word and you focus on being honorable and righteous, it is less important what others do and say. What truly matters is how faithfully you follow God's leading.

The Scriptures make it very clear what it means to be faithful. Someday we will stand before God, and He will welcome us into heaven by saying, "Come in! Well done, good and faithful servant!"

Prayer: Father God, You have said that we are to be faithful. We want to be known as faithful people who honor You. Amen.

Action: Be faithful in your actions today.

Being Passed Over

No one from the east or the west or from the desert
can exalt a man. But it is God who judges:
he brings one down, he exalts another.

PSALM 75:6-7

Nothing hurts like being passed over in life when you feel like you should have been selected for the team, chosen for the lead in the play, elected president of the club, or perhaps loved by that handsome football player you had a crush on in high school.

Today's verse is for all of us who have been left out. We all have wanted a certain position and didn't get it. We all have felt the sting of rejection, and there's perhaps only one thing more painful—watching our children be passed over for something on which they've set their hearts.

At such times, we are the one to whom they turn for consolation. You'll be called on to offer a lesson in how to have a stiff upper lip in times of disappointment. The wise mother will point her disappointed children to this powerful verse in Psalms.

God will lift up in His time, not ours. This is a hard, but very valuable, life lesson. God knows our hearts and yet is always wise in

His decisions. It is someone else's time right now, and it will help your children heal if they learn to rejoice with those who rejoice.

Their day will come, and it will be even sweeter for them, knowing that God has chosen the time for them to be picked. Live your life as an example of such patience and faith. Your family will witness your patience and your faith in the One who heals all wounds, even those caused by rejection and disappointment.

Prayer: Father God, take from me the desire for earthly recognition. Let me focus on the task, not on the reward. I know that You will lift me up in Your time—I trust You for that. Help me be a supportive mom when the time comes for me to comfort my child when he or she has been passed over. Amen.

Action: Be sure that you do not overlook those who need compassion and comfort. And when you feel overlooked and disappointed, turn your eyes to Jesus. You will see just how loved you are.

Take Time to Rest

Come to Me, all you who labor and are
heavy laden, and I will give you rest.
MATTHEW 11:28 NKJV

If you've ever gone to the Grand Canyon in Arizona, you have seen those burden-bearing donkeys that carry goods, people, and materials down to the canyon floor. They seem so small yet they carry such heavy loads. As you look at their swaybacks, it doesn't seem like they can continue one more step.

Jesus saw people that way—burdened and stressed, weighed down by the legalism and the legalistic demands the Pharisees had placed on them. No matter where they turned, some politician was telling them what to do or what not to do. Matthew 23:4 states:

> They bind heavy burdens, hard to bear, and lay them on
> men's shoulders; but they themselves will not move them
> with one of their fingers (NKJV).

We don't need religion that becomes an unbearable burden. We need rest from the terrible burden that sin and hopelessness create. That's why Jesus came! He came to give rest. By lifting the weight of sin from our shoulders, God opened the way for full and free living as He originally intended for us. To walk in obedience is never a burden—it's freedom.

It is also physically healthy to rest from the stresses of life. In order to live a long life, we must reduce the pressures in our lives. Prioritizing will help us cast off the hurry of today's technological age. Never in the history of mankind have we as people been under more pressure to perform. We are molded into thinking that we must have a perfect marriage, a perfect family, a perfect career, a perfect home. Because of this pressure, we will break if we don't relax.

Jesus says to come unto Him, and He will give us rest.

Prayer: Father God, we don't know what life would be like if You weren't alongside us to ease our burden. You have given me such great relief. Thank You! Amen.

Action: Get at least eight hours sleep every night. Don't shortchange your opportunities to restore your body, mind, and spirit through prayer, rest, and healthy living.

And It Was Good

And God saw that it was good.
GENESIS 1:10

*A*s women on the go, we often don't take the time to see, hear, and smell God's creation. We find ourselves being so busy that we don't take the precious time to study God's creation in its fullness.

Do you see evidence of God when you look around you? As I'm writing, the day is foggy where I live, and I can spy a single drop of dew on the leaves just beyond my kitchen window. With the sun breaking through the fog bank, this little drop of moisture is giving back to God a tiny sparkle of light that He sent from heaven.

Shakespeare spoke of "a gentle dew from heaven." He too must have taken a pause to look at a droplet of God's creation. He too must have been moved by the wonder of even such a small sample of God's work. I can fully understand how God looked at His creation—the earth and sky and waters—and confirmed that it was good. Glorious!

When you work at something and create something, do you take a moment to call it good? We get so busy and so focused on productivity and moving on to the next thing on the list that we forget to take that moment and honor God by offering up that creation to Him. Just like that little drop of dew, our efforts should reflect God's light back to heaven. It isn't prideful to be satisfied with your work. When you put your all into something, whether it is cooking a meal for your family, coordinating a volunteer work party at your church, painting a room, or completing a work project that took a lot of research and diligence, it is important to take a moment and praise God, celebrate, or simply take a moment to rest before you start something new. Slow down and wait until the Lord tells us "it is good."

Prayer: God, it is so good just to know that You created the droplets left by fog, so good to know You care about the smallest elements of life. Amen.

Action: Spend time resting in God's creation. Sit on your front porch or in your backyard for 10 minutes today. Take in the sounds and smells and beauty of nature. Thank God for all that you see and breathe deeply! You'll feel like you took a vacation.

Our Father in heaven,
hallowed be your name,
your kingdom come,
your will be done
on earth as it is in heaven.
MATTHEW 6:9-10

The Lord's Prayer is one of the most precious prayers of the Christian faith. And it all begins with this adoration of God: Our Father in heaven.

God tenderly invites us to believe that He is truly our Father, and we are truly His children, so that we may ask of Him in all cheerfulness and confidence, as dear children ask of their dear father. We can all go through periods when we act more like stubborn children than willing ones. We want to try and do it all ourselves because we like the control, and we think that puts us truly in charge. Of course, it really doesn't. Such behavior just puts us further away from God's direction and will for us. Life actually becomes more out of control, chaotic even. And we never have the peace that comes from resting in our Father's wisdom and truth.

James 4:2 states, "You do not have, because you do not ask God."

We try many ways to cope with the stresses of life. Often we escape into work, leisure time, body toning, and exercise, and even many kinds of addictions. Often these escapes look like a way to survive, but behaviors turned to as responses to stress—even those with religious trappings—are not the solution. God wants us to boldly approach His throne and commit our requests, our adoration, our thanks, and our supplications to Him in the form of prayer.

God Himself is the only one who can direct us to live life as He meant it to be.

Since God is so near to us, we can approach Him in a very personal way. When we open our prayer with the phrase "Our Father," we acknowledge that the answers of life lie beyond our abilities, our looks, our social position, and our economic status.

We admit that our might is not enough to live the fullest life that God intended for us. We have to be very brave to admit we need someone bigger than we are. But we can call upon the Father in confidence, knowing that we are His children and that He hears us.

We gain strength and confidence when we call on God by name and admit that we need Him for our every need and that we are helpless without Him.

Prayer: My Father who art in Heaven, thank You for allowing me to come to Your throne. I need You today and every day. I am so privileged to be Your child. You show me how to love, how to forgive, and how to rest in God's peace. Amen.

Action: Go to your heavenly Father with your every need. You have God's attention, what do you want to say to Him? What hopes do you want to express?

When Faith Seems Lost

Wives, fit in with your husbands' plans; for then
if they refuse to listen when you talk to them
about the Lord, they will be won by your
respectful, pure behavior. Your godly lives will
speak to them better than any words.

1 PETER 3:1 TLB

Bob and I were hosting a radio talk show in Southern California when a lady called in and asked, "How do you love a husband who isn't a Christian?" I thought for a moment then replied, "The same way you would love a husband who is a Christian."

Too often husbands who aren't believers—and even some who are—feel they are in competition with Jesus for the love of their wives. That is definitely not how to love your husband, whatever his faith! These men often give up on their marriage relationships, believing they can't compete for their wives' devotion against someone as good as Jesus. Wives do indeed need to love God with all their hearts, souls, and minds (Matthew 22:37), but they are also to love their husbands—even when their husbands have hardened their hearts or strayed from the Lord.

Standing by your man when his heart is hard against God is difficult but it may be easier if you understand a few things first:

- Realize that you are not responsible for your husband's salvation.
- You are not appointed to be the change agent in his life.
- Your husband's salvation is between God and him.

Are you relieved to discover that your husband's salvation isn't your responsibility? I meet so many women who take on this responsibility and then feel like failures time after time. Often they turn those feelings of failure into more worry and even anger toward their husbands. And that, in turn, causes them to stop modeling godly, loving behavior to their husbands, and it makes their marriages miserable!

So ultimately, what is your role if your husband's heart isn't open to the Lord? Your role is to love him. Today's Scripture verse gives very clear direction on what your role should be. Let those words encourage you to stand by your man—and recognize that fitting in with his plans won't always be easy!

Prayer: Father God, give me the courage to step out in faith for Your word. Let me be willing to trust and obey. Amen.

Action: Ask your husband if he has three or four specific needs that you can work toward satisfying. Pray over this list and ask God to direct your path in satisfying these needs.

*D*on't Forget the Past

From childhood you have known the
Holy Scriptures, which are able to make you wise
for salvation through faith which is in Christ Jesus.

2 TIMOTHY 3:15 NKJV

*H*ow many of us have lamented things in our past? Sometimes you meet people who dwell on the past so much it is as if they are living there permanently. We all have actions, words, mistakes, and sins that blemish our personal histories, but we mustn't forget that when you know and love the Lord, your past is an amazing miracle...it brought you to the place of faith and salvation.

God knows your past and of course knows your long or short lists of transgressions, but what He sees is the new creation that you are through Him. What He notices is your faithfulness now, and your desire to follow His heart. God has loved you and known you from the very beginning. He's just excited that you are here today.

Because of this miracle we are here today—and not by accident. We are here for a purpose. Have you taken time to consider what this purpose might be?

In Scripture, we are challenged not to forget what matters most. Paul writes in 2 Timothy 1:6-8:

I remind you to fan into flame the gift of God, which is in you through the laying on of my hands. For God did not give us a spirit of timidity, but a spirit of power, of love and of discipline.

In these latter days we as believers will be called on to stand up and give witness to Jesus and what He has done through history. We are told that during the last days men will

- ignore God
- love stuff
- use people
- play religious games
- be boastful and proud
- see children being disobedient to parents
- be ungrateful
- consider nothing sacred

This is certainly a list for today. But every day I try to remember the lessons of history to remind myself to...

- Follow the examples God has given: "But you, Timothy, certainly know what I teach, and how I live, and what my purpose in life is. You know my faith, my patience, my love, and my endurance" (2 Timothy 3:10 NLT).

- Remain in God's Word: "You must remain faithful to the things you have been taught. You know they are true, for you know you can trust those who taught you. You have been taught the holy Scriptures from childhood, and they have given you the wisdom to receive the salvation that comes by trusting in Christ Jesus. All Scripture is inspired by God and is useful to teach us what is true and to make us realize what is wrong in our lives. It corrects us when we are wrong and teaches us to do what is right.

God uses it to prepare and equip his people to do every good work" (2 Timothy 3:14-17 NLT).

- Complete my calling: "We will all stand personally before the judgment seat of God. For the Scriptures say, 'As surely as I live,' says the Lord, 'every knee will bow to me and every tongue will confess allegiance to God.' Yes, each of us will have a personal account to God" (Romans 14:10-12 NLT).

Biblical history lets me rest assured that God has a master plan for all of history, including my personal history. Though we might not know the master plan, we can know that God's thoughts are bigger than our thoughts. I'm not capable of understanding every event in history, but because I know who God is, I can be at peace with all situations. I want to know my past so I can know the future.

Prayer: Father God, give me a desire to know my history to better understand the present and trust You for the future. Give me a desire to reach out and find my purpose in life. Amen.

Action: Take time to think through your history so that you can thank God for His faithfulness. Ask for forgiveness for any sins that remain and then release it all to God.

Is It Mud or Beauty?

If anything is excellent or praiseworthy—
think about such things.

Philippians 4:8

One Sunday morning, we were going to the airport in Maui, Hawaii, and it began to rain. We were surprised when the shuttle bus driver said excitedly, "This is a day for celebration." When she noticed our expressions of curiosity, she explained that, in Hawaii, if rain falls on your wedding, it will bring good luck. We looked at each other and both agreed that in Southern California if it rained on your wedding it would be a disaster. Strange how people look at things differently.

On one rainy day, a woman overheard another person say, "What miserable weather!" The woman looked out of her apartment window to see a big, fat robin using a nearby puddle of water for a bathtub. It was having a wonderful time splashing water everywhere. She thought, "Miserable for whom?"

Another example of such diverse perspective was when a young boy watched an artist paint a picture of a muddy river. The boy told the artist he didn't like the picture because there was too much mud in it. The artist did admit there was mud, but what he saw was the beautiful colors and contrasts of the light against the dark. There are different ways to view the same scene, the same moment, and the same circumstance.

Mud or beauty—which do we look for as we travel through life? Do you tend to see the mud and a great deal of it as you look at the day ahead or even as you review the past? Is it possible that there are gentle hues and surprising colors blended in as well? Take another look at the day, the moment, or the memory and discover where there is beauty.

As Paul taught in today's passage, we are to look for and think about things that are true, honest, just, pure, lovely, of good report, and things with virtue. Look for the best and see the beautiful in everything each day. We have often heard the expression, "What you see is what you get." That's exactly what life is all about. Look beyond the mud and see the beautiful contrasts between the light and the dark. This is the way to get the best out of life.

The next time you are moaning and groaning because you want something beautiful, shiny, bright, and lovely in your life, take a moment of prayer and observation to notice how God already has placed something truly beautiful in your life—even in the midst of a rainy season!

    Prayer: Father God, let us look at life with a perspective focused on seeing Your beauty in our surroundings. Amen.

    Action: Watch for a robin splashing in a pool of water.

Good News Before Bad News

All Scripture is inspired by God and profitable for teaching,
for reproof, for correction, for training in righteousness; so that
the man of God may be adequate, equipped for every good work.

2 TIMOTHY 3:16-17 NASB

Some days I wake up and reach for the morning paper or turn on the TV to catch the latest news. After all, it's important to be well informed about world events. But after a few short days of this, I'm reminded of a saying that I once heard, "Read the Good News before you read the bad news."

That's absolutely right. Why would any busy woman, already carrying the important responsibilities of her family, want to start the day off with the bad news that always seems to make the biggest headlines before she reads the Good News of Scripture?

When I start off my day reading and reflecting on God's Word, my day is energized, and I handle my responsibilities, choices, and emotions with God's wisdom leading the way. As I look back over the years, I know that the times when I skipped my morning moments with the Lord were also the times when I encountered frustration and experienced a lack of focus. I seemed to move along from one small crisis to the next, without peace or purpose.

Even if logic tells you that you have no more time or energy to set aside for *anything,* trust your heart and turn to the Good News each morning—it enriches your life with goodness.

Prayer: Father God, I pray for the energy and discipline it will take to commit to time with You each day. It is what I long for...please, gently urge my spirit to enter Your presence. I want to draw from the source of good news before I face the busy day. Grow my passion for this daily activity, Lord.

Action: Look at your upcoming week and plan a day to start this refreshing ritual. What time will you commit to? Start your day just 15 minutes earlier and soon this time of solitude and feasting on words of goodness will become a great blessing in your life.

How to Love the Rich Life

The sun rises with a scorching wind and withers the grass;
and its flower falls off and the beauty of its appearance
is destroyed; so too the rich man in the midst
of his pursuits will fade away.

JAMES 1:11

One of our young grandchildren asked Papa Bob, "Are you rich?"

"Yes, in the Lord," he answered. "No, Papa, I mean really rich?" he insisted. He wanted to know if his grandpa was monetarily rich. The good old capitalist word: money.

Regardless of where most of us are on the financial barometer of life, we are rich compared to someone—especially when we consider the world's population. Just by living in America we are rich. If you don't think so, just ask any of the many immigrants, legal and illegal, who come to this country every year.

And being rich carries a lot of responsibility. When one is wealthy, that person usually has power over things and people. In 1 Timothy 6:10 we read, "For the love of money is a root of all sorts of evil, and some by longing for it have wandered away from the faith and pierced themselves with many griefs."

The writer isn't saying that being rich is wrong, but that the love of money is the basis for all kinds of evil. We need to examine our attitude toward material wealth. And the result of that examination should determine how we live—because how we live communicates what our concept of wealth is to our children.

A simple lifestyle (as opposed to an ostentatious, wasteful lifestyle) lets our children know that whatever riches we have aren't the most important priority in our life. Instead, let's be good stewards of the gifts God has given us—giving generously to others in need, both of our time and our financial resources. And bring your children into discussions about how and where to give to others.

Exhibit that your security and peace doesn't come from your bank account, but from your relationship with Christ. Live in such a way that your children will understand that your riches in heaven are more exciting than your riches on earth. Teach them that it's more blessed to give than to receive.

Prayer: God, You are a provider of abundance. May our family be found worthy to be a steward of all Your resources. I thank You for the riches You have given us. Amen.

Action: What are your true spiritual riches. Think on this. Make a list. Take time spending, sharing, and passing along these treasures.

Pursue Peace

Peace I leave with you, My peace I give to you.
JOHN 14:27 NKJV

The world likes peace. They like the idea of it and they like to talk about it. Peace symbols adorn buses, backpacks, and bumper stickers, and peace itself is pleaded for everywhere and in every language. Lasting peace is certainly what we need, and isn't it true that it is also what we crave? However, most people are looking for it in the world or the world's offerings. And they often equate happiness or fulfillment of their desires as peace. But peace defined by the fruit of the Spirit is an assured quietness of the soul. It is the opposite of our earthly struggles, and it is best described as a "wellness between oneself and God." It isn't about reaching career goals or having life easy—it is about a healthy relationship with your Creator.

The peace that God gives is built on the awareness that we all have purpose and cause for existing. As we mature in our spiritual nature and learn what this life is all about, we discover that only our heavenly Father can give us a lasting calmness within. Once we realize this, we no longer toss and turn, trying to find answers to our daily struggles. We have reconciled with God through Jesus, His Son, that life has meaning and we are created in God's image. We know the Alpha and the Omega. We finally know who we are. We have inner tranquility of mind, soul, and spirit. There is a calmness to our presence that is recognizable as God's peace.

When our lives reflect God's love and joy, those around us will be lifted up by our outward expression of this fruit of the Spirit.

Prayer: Father God, may we continue to be willing and patient to develop our lives toward the precious virtue of peace. Amen.

Action: Live in peace with one another.

We Are Created Differently

*An unlearned carpenter once said, "There is very
little difference between one man and another.
What little difference there is, is very important."*
WILLIAM JAMES

*Whatever you do, work at it with all your heart, as
working for the Lord, not for men, since you know
that you will receive an inheritance from the Lord as
a reward. It is the Lord Christ you are serving.*
COLOSSIANS 3:23-24 NKJV

Though some want to argue that there are not any differences between the sexes, those of us who are married know otherwise! It is evident to Bob and me that men and women are different—and those differences are much deeper than the obvious physical ones. What circumstances have caused you to realize just how differently you and your husband think? What situations have brought to the foreground the differences between how you and your husband act? Despite what the world says, men and women are different.

Today's culture invites women to expect men to think and act as they do. In a marriage, these unrealistic expectations can result in disappointment and cries such as, "What's wrong with our marriage? He doesn't even care!" Are you sure your husband doesn't care? You may simply have come up against the fact that a man will show that he cares differently than a woman shows she cares. How we express our love is just one of the many differences between men and women.

What can a good wife do in the face of these differences? She can acknowledge and accept how her husband is different from her. Such acceptance comes more easily when we remember that God made man and woman different. We also need to be aware that some of the differences are due to our individual strengths and weaknesses. You and your husband each entered into marriage with certain strengths and certain weaknesses.

Too often male-female differences are at the root of marital problems. This friction is due not so much to the fact that men and women are physically, emotionally, psychologically, and culturally different from one another, but from the fact that we don't understand those differences or work to accommodate them in our relationships. A marriage grows and thrives when a husband and wife understand and accept that God has designed them to be different and complementary.

Prayer: Father God, let me realize that my husband isn't wrong, but just different from me. Let me know that his differences complement my differences. Amen.

Action: Love is not all that simple, it is an act that must be learned. We all can learn to love.

$\mathscr{F}$ear Not

When you pass through the waters,
I will be with you.
ISAIAH 43:2

$\mathscr{D}$o you know that it's against God's character to give you a promise and not to keep it? We live in a culture where many people make promises that they do not keep. God is not like that. If He says it—He will do it. Don't let the world define for you what a promise is. If you do, you will be confused by God's Word. He (God) cannot break a promise.

Notice that Isaiah says "when"—not "if." Sooner or later, all of us will go through deep waters. If you aren't right at the moment, you eventually will. Stand in line—your time will come.

When we are young or when life is treating us well, it is hard to think about the woes of life. They might happen to others, but surely not to me or my family. I vividly remember when my doctor announced to me and my family, "Emilie, you have cancer!" I was devastated. I had read and heard that others had cancer, but surely not me. I couldn't believe what I heard. Me? Surely not me!

But if the Lord grants us an abundance of years, we will all experience the woes of life. This passage of Scripture described my status in this fight for my life. I was passing through the deep waters, wading through the rivers, and walking through the fire.

During this time, I claimed God's promises:

- God is with me.
- The rivers aren't sweeping over me.
- The fires aren't burning me.
- God is calling me by name, and I will fear no evil.

Another passage of Scripture that I had read many times came alive to me. Not until I was walking in the valley of the shadow of death did I appreciate what was being taught.

> Consider it all joy, my brethren, when you encounter various trials, knowing that the testing of your faith produces endurance. And let endurance have its perfect result that you may be perfect and complete, lacking in nothing.
>
> —JAMES 1:2-4 NASB

It has now been 12 long years since my doctor told me that I had cancer. If anyone would have told me that I could or would be able to endure such a journey—I would have said, "No, I can't." However, God had a different lesson for me to learn when He declared, "Yes, you can!" Friends will ask me, "How did you do it?" My reply is, "A day at a time and many days and hours at a time."

If you find yourself going down a dark road, I tell you, "Fear not."

Prayer: Father God, You know that I am not a brave lady, but by Your grace and mercy You have given me the strength to endure. Thank You for that courage. Amen.

Action: Step out in faith and trust God's promises.

Today Is a Gift

*We were under great pressure, far beyond our
ability to endure, so that we despaired even of life.*
2 CORINTHIANS 1:8

Does today's verse sound like your life? Well, maybe not quite as despairing, I hope. But your complex role as a busy woman—especially a busy mom—is almost beyond description. Without a doubt you have one of the most difficult, demanding, and taxing job descriptions in the world.

When I'm out shopping, I see moms with little children, and I quickly think back to the day when I had the same responsibilities. For all of us, whether we are parents or not, the ever-increasing pressures and stresses of living are sometimes intense, making it almost impossible for us to live the abundant life we all seek. Dad is pressured on the job. Profit margins are getting smaller, and competition is getting more fierce. While striving for excellence at work, Dad also wants to be a loving husband, father, and leader of his family. Maybe you face the same stresses of being in the workforce. What big responsibilities we carry at different times in our lives!

What stresses do you face regarding the management of your household—keeping the children focused, satisfying your husband, or maintaining a proper balance in your life? As Christians we can endure these stresses successfully if we view life's pressures as opportunities for us to demonstrate God's power. How we respond to our various pressures helps shape us into the person we will be tomorrow. If it takes all these stresses to make us into the person God has designed us to be, then all these uncomfortable situations will have made it all worthwhile. These efforts, trials, challenges, and blessings of responsibility are God's means for revealing His strength as you tackle the duties you face daily.

> Yesterday is history, tomorrow is a mystery, today is God's gift, that's why we call it the present.
>
> —JOAN RIVERS

Look upon today as a gift. No matter what pressures the day brings—it truly is a gift for you. With each inconvenience you meet, may you realize that this too is merely a building block for whom God wants you to become.

Prayer: Father, no one enjoys the pressures of life, but if I look at them as teaching tools for whom I am becoming, then I say, "Bring it on." Amen.

Action: Today when you feel the stress piling on, consider how you can respond in God's strength. You will discover the amazing things God is wanting to do in and through your circumstance.

To Let It Grow

Is your life full of difficulties and temptations?
Then be happy, for when the way is rough,
your patience has a chance to grow.

JAMES 1:2-3 TLB

Throughout Scripture, we read of victory over troubles and suffering. Helmut Thielicke, a great German pastor and theologian, testified to this kind of victory during the horrors of World War II. "We live by God's surprises," he proclaimed after he had personally suffered under the Nazis. As a pastor, he wrote to young soldiers about to die; he comforted mothers, fathers, and children after the bombs killed their loved ones. He preached magnificent sermons week after week as bombs blew apart his church and the lives and dreams of his parishioners. He spoke of God not only looking in love at His suffering people, weeping with them as they were surrounded by flames, but of God's hand reaching into the flames to help them, His own hand scorched by the fires. From the depths of suffering and the wanton destruction caused by the Nazi regime, Thielicke held out a powerful Christian hope. To Germans disillusioned by the easily manipulated faith of their fathers, he quoted philosopher Peter Wust: "The great things happen to those who pray. But we learn to pray best in suffering."

Prayer, suffering, joy, and the surprises of God...they are all tightly enmeshed. But many people shrink from suffering, afraid that it will kill their joy and keep them from experiencing "great things." When we are rightly related to God, life is full of joyful uncertainty and expectancy. We do not know what God is going to do next; He packs our lives with surprises all the time. Prayer becomes the lens through which we begin to see from God's perspective.

Prayer: Father God, I want to live life in expectation of Your surprises. I want to stand on tiptoe to see Your mysteries unveiled for me. Amen.

Action: Stand on your tiptoes to see what God is going to do next in your life.

Engraved on Your Heart

Her children arise and call her blessed;
her husband also, and he praises her.

PROVERBS 31:28

The famous thirty-first chapter of Proverbs is a portrait of the kind of godly woman I want to be. She is hard working, nurturing, creative. She has a good business sense as well as a finely tuned sense of balance and a delight in her role as wife and mother. Most important she is a "woman who fears the LORD." And what is her reward for all her efforts? "Her children arise and call her blessed; her husband also, and he praises her" (verse 28).

Such a reward would warm any woman's heart. I know I love it whenever my husband, Bob, and the children praise me and "call me blessed"! But I am also aware that many of you are godly women who pattern your life after biblical principles but do not receive praise from anyone. Many times you may feel or say, "What's the use? No one appreciates me."

Oh, there have been times in my life when I haven't felt appreciated, but God has taught me through these void periods in my life. I began to realize that God was dealing with me on the level of my motivations and my expectations. He wanted me to do whatever I did to please Him, not my husband or my children or anyone else.

When I began to stop expecting people to react in a certain way, I began to act out of proper motivation. I was aiming to please God, not expecting certain behavior from family and friends.

Do you know what began to happen? I stopped expecting praise from my family, but I started getting it! My praise came about when my family was free to be themselves. However, I'm not nearly as hungry for compliments as I once was. I find I am satisfied because I am becoming more used to responding in a godly way to life and its many situations. I have become more aware of who I really am as God's child and why I am here: to grow closer to Him and learn His way of doing things. In the process, I have become far less dependent on other people to feel worthwhile.

> She gets up while it is still dark; she provides food for her family, and portions for her servant girls.
>
> —Proverbs 31:15

In talking to hundreds of women each year, I find that they are vainly trying to find the answers to those same two questions: "Who am I?" and "Why am I here?" If God's answer to these two questions of life is not yet engraved on your heart, I pray that you will set out on a journey to be satisfied with your answers. Go to God's Scripture, talk to a godly friend, attend a Bible-teaching church, set aside a part of each day to talk to God in prayer. If you seek sincerely, God will show you the traits of the godly woman He created you to be. Then step out in obedience, depending on Jesus. As you do, the beauty of godliness will begin to shine in your life.

As women, we have the wonderful opportunity to let our lives sparkle with God's love—if we let Him. Almighty God is our guide and shepherd and will give us the spirit of godliness to complete our search for who am I and why am I here.

Prayer: Father God, You give me hope when I am discouraged. You lift me out of my disappointments when my expectations aren't realized. May I learn to look to You rather than to others for my approval. Amen.

Action: Who are you trying to please, God or others? Maybe you need to refocus your direction. If so, begin today.

Your Comfort and Security

*Peace I leave with you; my peace I give you.
I do not give to you as the world gives. Do not let
your hearts be troubled and do not be afraid.*

JOHN 14:27

When our first grandchild was born, her parents named her Christine Marie—Christine from her mother's middle name and Marie from my middle name. As my namesake, I'm very proud of Christine Marie. She is our only granddaughter among four grandsons.

From flannel fabric I made her a pink-printed blanket with some small roses. The blanket was edged with a pink satin binding. It was only about eight inches by eight inches, very small. Well, it quickly became her security blankie while she sucked her thumb. The blankie got twisted, wadded up, and smoothed by little Christine Marie. She was finally able to pull loose an end and twist the threads around her fingers.

Christine loved her pink rosebud blankie. It gave her comfort when she wasn't feeling well, softness when she was afraid, and security when she felt alone. Then one day five years later the blankie got folded and put in an envelope that she tucked away in her dresser drawer. From time to time she still pulls out the envelope to look at the rosebud flannel security blanket.

Jesus is like the security blanket that Christine Marie once held close to her—only today she has almighty God our Heavenly Father, God the Son, and God the Holy Spirit to hold tight to.

As today's Scripture states, Jesus gives us peace in the midst of the storms of life; when we are going through that difficult tornado of a broken marriage, the death of a dream, financial troubles, childless pain, ill health, or all the other trials we encounter in just living out our daily lives.

Christ is our security blanket when we are afraid and feel fearful of tomorrow.

My mama used to tell me in the middle of the night when I needed to go to the bathroom but was afraid of the dark, "Be afraid, but go anyway." Today I know I can go because I have my Lord who is with me wherever I go. When I'm weak and upset, He holds me and comforts my heart.

Of course, Jesus is more than just a security blanket. He's our Comforter, our Savior, the Messiah, the Alpha and Omega, the Almighty, the Everlasting, our bright and morning star, our Counselor, our strength, our Redeemer, our peace, our High Priest, our cornerstone, our foundation, our master builder, and a hundred other necessities for us.

It's time to give our blanket over to Jesus and allow Him to be our Master Comforter.

Prayer: God, thank You for letting me put away my old childhood security blanket and for giving me faith to trust You in all situations. Let me, by example, lead my family to do the same. Amen.

Action: Take comfort in the security of God's promises and in His purpose for your life. Learn to rest in the peace of Christ more every day.

$\mathscr{E}$ncourage Your Pastor

Remember your leaders, who spoke the word of God to you.
HEBREWS 13:7

$\mathscr{A}$ pastor friend of ours recalls a large Promise Keepers gathering in Los Angeles where the master of ceremonies requested that all the pastors in the crowd come onto the stadium floor. As thousands of faithful pastors came forward, the remaining sixty thousand men in the stadium stood up and started to clap, shout, and whistle. The roar of the men became deafening. The applause lasted for at least ten minutes. Recognition for the pastors' faithfulness in ministry was long overdue. As the emcee finished giving honor to these servants of God, the audience gave another standing ovation. Our friend said tears came down his cheeks as he heard such approval from those in attendance.

> He has honor if he holds himself to an ideal of conduct though it is inconvenient, unprofitable, or dangerous to do so.
>
> —WALTER LIPPMANN

Have you taken the time to encourage your pastor for his role in feeding the flock of God and overseeing their spiritual welfare? We often take for granted that week after week our ministers will study and prepare a sermon that will reach us with God's truth. Often they feel unappreciated. Though they aren't looking for praise, they do need the encouragement of those who are helped by their dedication to your church.

Prayer: Father God, thank You for giving us a wonderful pastor who encourages our walk with You. Please bless his life and family today.

Action: Make a dozen cookies, tie a bow around the packaging, and take this treat to his office at church.

God's Grace Is Sufficient

*The Spirit helps us in our weakness. We do not know
what we ought to pray for, but the Spirit himself
intercedes for us with groans that words cannot express.*

ROMANS 8:26

When I don't have the strength to utter my desires to heaven, God's grace will hear without me speaking the words. God understands even our groanings. Our tongues don't have to speak words before He hears them. Parents often know what's in their children's mind without them even talking. Likewise a spouse instantaneously knows what the other is thinking and oftentimes finishes a sentence of the mate. God is like this with us.

The Holy Spirit is the alpha and omega of our prayers. He knows the beginning and the end. He knows our hearts and can discern our troubles and pleas even when we ourselves are struggling to know what to pray specifically.

During many of my stays at hospitals I often didn't know what to pray for. My Bob and I didn't always have the knowledge to properly understand our situation. Oh, yes, we asked questions, but the explanations weren't decoded for our ears. These large multisyllable medical terms were too difficult for our layman ears to grasp. To be honest with you, there were times when we were too tired and stressed to even feel like praying.

However, during these void times, we knew God would redeem our energy, and that He would give us the "right words" for the moment. These were great prayer sessions! We entered with little and exited with joy and satisfaction. How could it be? We were so confused, but God gave us order.

Don't be fearful to pray when you feel the same way we felt. The Holy Spirit will renew your desire for prayer, and He will give you words to speak. God's grace is sufficient for all our needs.

Prayer: Father God, just knowing that You will intercede for me when I don't have the power or words to say is so reassuring. Thanks for knowing me that well. Amen.

Action: When you pray today, really think about how your words are received and known by God.

> Do all the good you can
> By all the means you can,
> In all the ways you can,
> In all the places you can,
> At all the times you can,
> To all the people you can,
> As long as ever you can.
>
> —JOHN WESLEY

Be Joyful

These things I have spoken to you,
that My joy may remain in you,
and that your joy may be full.
JOHN 15:11 NKJV

Is your glass half-empty or half full? How you answer that basic question of life will reveal your joy level. If you answer half-empty you probably lack joy in your life. However, if your answer is half full your joy reading would rate pretty high.

People like to be around individuals who radiate joy in their presence. And when people have little joy in their lives, they often have few friendships.

Many times we expect the fruit of joy to bring us unlimited happiness and fun times. Yet when we read the Scriptures, we are encouraged to reflect on what it really means to have a joyful heart. Happiness and fun are good in themselves, but they come and go. Joy, however, is felt beyond our circumstances. Joy exists even when times are difficult because it is part of the attitude we have toward life's experiences. It is a treasure of the heart, the comfort of knowing God's intimate presence.

Find joy in simplicity, self-respect, and indifference to what lies between virtue and vice. Love the human race. Follow the divine.

—AURELIUS

As we view the events of our lives, we can choose to be resentful toward God for letting certain things happen to us or we can choose an attitude of gratitude and a commitment to joy. Joy is our best choice. We have joy when we are serving God and doing what He wants for our lives. We have joy when we learn to take circumstances and the ups and downs of life in stride and to use all situations to bring glory to Jesus. We lighten our load in life and draw others to us by having a joyful heart. When we have joy in the Lord, we begin to see life from God's point of view. We will realize that things have never looked so beautiful, so peaceful, so amazing. The joy of the Lord is truly our strength.

The psalmist expresses this concept so well when he writes:

"Shout for joy to the LORD, all the earth. Worship the LORD with gladness; come before him with joyful songs."

—PSALM 100:1-2

Prayer: Father God, thank You for giving me an attitude of joy. I can truly share that having a glass half full is more rewarding than having a glass that is half empty. Amen.

Action: Find joy in your most difficult situation.

$\mathscr{B}$e a Woman of Trust

Trust in the LORD with all your heart and lean not
on your own understanding; in all your ways
acknowledge him, and he will make your paths straight.

PROVERBS 3:5-6

$\mathscr{I}$ve heard many husbands and wives discuss how difficult it is for them to trust one another. While many couples might depend on one another, they struggle with actually trusting and working with each other toward common goals. Are they stubborn, mean, uncaring, apathetic? No. These are good folks who have forgotten a key factor in their relationships...they are supposed to be trusting God in every situation. That is how a couple can work together toward a common objective, a purposed life, and a faithful relationship.

When you and your husband truly begin working together as a team, you can accomplish so much more than you could ever accomplish alone. Sometimes I need a masculine point of view, and sometimes Bob needs to see the feminine viewpoint. We balance out each other. I'm a better woman because of him, and he's a better man because of me. I don't have his strengths and he doesn't have my strengths. We've learned to let each other achieve satisfaction and success in our areas of strength.

One of the things I do in our marriage is let Bob know I appreciate all the ways he protects our family. Through the years I've affirmed him in that role. But as with most valuable truths, I had to learn to do that. Early in our marriage we lived near a busy intersection with no stoplights. We had to negotiate it every day. Trying to turn onto that busy thoroughfare from our street made a nervous wreck out of me. The cars came so fast—from both directions—and we had to merge quickly with speeding traffic. To make the left turn we needed, we often had to wait a long time for appropriate gaps in the traffic.

I'll admit that I'm a more cautious driver than Bob. And in situations where I would typically wait for a better opening, he stomped on the accelerator and darted into the flow of traffic. Frankly, it scared me, and I used to grip the passenger side armrest and close my eyes tightly when he took off. We've never had any real problems or any accidents related to Bob's quick-reflex driving style, but it frightened me and I told him so.

Finally, after weeks of this, it dawned on me that I was basically telling him I didn't trust him. Being a man, that bothered Bob. So I swallowed hard and resolved to change my behavior at that intersection the next time we approached it. And that's just what I did.

Instead of tensing up and looking quickly back and forth or closing my eyes, I forced myself to relax and leave the driving and my fate in his hands.

> Trust men and they will be true to you; treat them greatly
> and they will show themselves great.
>
> —Ralph Waldo Emerson

After he slipped the car smoothly into what looked to me like an incredibly small gap in traffic, I said nothing, trying to be the very picture of relaxation and ease. I'll always remember that moment. Bob shot me a quick glance and said, "Well? You didn't say anything to me this time."

I replied, "You know, honey, I trust you."

"Hmmm," was all he said. But I could see my words had an effect. There have been other situations in driving when I saw things one way and he saw things in another, and because he was driving, we went with his instincts rather than mine. Yes, sometimes it's very difficult to sit there, trust him, and submit to his decision making. But that is exactly what God asks me to do as his wife.

If we can't yield to our husbands' leadership in small situations, how obedient will we be to God in really big situations? This doesn't imply that as women and wives we're inferior to our husbands in any way. No, it simply means God established a certain hierarchy or chain of command in the family, and He promised to bless those who obey and follow His Word.

Prayer: Father God, may I turn my heart to You and walk in all Your ways and keep Your commands. Amen.

Action: In some way that only a wife can do, express to your husband that you love and respect him.

Live Life on Purpose

Whether you eat or drink or whatever you do,
do it all for the glory of God.
1 CORINTHIANS 10:31

Have you ever been challenged to live life on purpose? If not, I challenge you now. Especially your life as a mother. God has plans for your children—and for you. It's not His will that we coast through life casually and aimlessly. Life's far too short for that.

God has placed us here on earth for a reason. And when we discover that reason and live our life to that godly end, we find true satisfaction.

I've been very fortunate to meet a lot of wonderful people. All walks of life, all colors, all denominations—some with no denominations. But the ones I count the most wise are those who understand that everything is to be done to the glory of God. They directed their lives toward a purpose—and that simple difference has given them the impetus and energy to succeed where many others have failed.

In ancient days, all the craftsmen, artisans, and musicians proclaimed their godly purpose in life by what they produced. That's why the great classics of the world reflect a spiritual tribute to who God is. Through their endeavor, their work was beautiful and thus eternal.

In the twenty-first century few artists are creating works that will attain "classic" status. Why? Because most composers, sculptors, writers, and artists don't create their work to glorify God. Often what was once ugly is now considered beautiful, and what was beautiful has become ugly. Just look at our contemporary music, art, theater, cinema, and literature to see how we have strayed.

God's desire is for you and for each member of your family to be purposeful human beings. To work toward meaningful goals and experience the joy of achievement. So learn to live your life on purpose, and teach your children to do the same. If necessary, write out some obtainable goals and work toward them. Read books that motivate you toward your goal or that help you set worthy goals.

Above all, pray for God's guidance in your "on-purpose" life.

Prayer: Creator, give me purposeful direction on living a life that will glorify You. I'm tired of "shooting from the hip"; I'm weary of coasting. Help me choose wisely and move toward the right goals. Amen.

Action: Watch and pray over your family members and ask that God's guidance and purpose be revealed to them. Pray the same for yourself.

Knowing God's Timetable

There is a time for everything and a season for every activity under heaven…He has made everything beautiful in its time. He has also set eternity in the hearts of men; yet they cannot fathom what God has done from beginning to end.

ECCLESIASTES 3:1,11

One great accomplishment in life is learning to find rest in our appointed time—relishing the joys and challenges that come with each new stage of living. These include the excitement and possibilities of youth, the satisfaction and fulfillment of maturity, and the wisdom and patience of later years. As we advance in age, though we see our youth and its aspirations flee by, we gather wonderful memories to cherish and new lessons to learn. We anticipate, more and more eagerly, the time of being with the Lord for eternity.

I have had the privilege of writing seventy books over the last 25 years, and as I look back over this span of time, I can see how my various books are about the seasons of life I'm experiencing as I write them. I've covered subjects like marriage, home management, children, tea parties, grandchildren, how to be an effective grandparent, surviving cancer, etc.

I have learned that God has a master plan for my life, and I am comforted in knowing I live by His timetable. I have already experienced so many of His seasons—each one good in its own way. Why shouldn't I expect the next stage to be good as well?

God is the potter and I am the clay. He will mold me and make me in His own way. Remain pliable and flexible so God can mold you more easily.

Prayer: Father God, You are my friend. I know that You work all things together for my good. Help me to be more flexible. Amen.

Action: In your journal, write down five memories you are thankful for.

God's Idea of Intimacy

Marriage should be honored by all, and the
marriage bed kept pure, for God will judge
the adulterer and all the sexually immoral.

HEBREWS 13:4

The Bible's teaching on marriage has helped me learn about God's master plan for husbands and wives. One of the most important passages I have discovered is found in 1 Corinthians 7:1-5 (NASB):

> It is good for a man not to touch a woman. But because of immoralities, each man is to have his own wife, and each woman is to have her own husband. The husband must fulfill his duty to his wife, and likewise also the wife to her husband. The wife does not have authority over her own body, but the husband does; and likewise also the husband does not have authority over his own body, but the wife does. Stop depriving one another, except by agreement for a time, so that you may devote yourselves to prayer, and come together again lest Satan tempt you because of your lack of self-control.

These verses provide four solid guidelines for couples who desire love and intimacy in their relationship.

1. Be faithful to one person. God's Word clearly commands us to be faithful to one spouse (Exodus 20:14; Matthew 5:27-32).

2. Be available to each other. A husband is to give of himself to fulfill his wife's needs, and the wife is to give of herself to fulfill her husband's needs. We are to freely ask for and give affection to one another.

3. Submit to each other. Be willing to submit to your mate's sexual desires and needs.

4. Keep on meeting your mate's sexual needs. Paul notes that the only exception to this guideline is taking time for prayer and fasting. Other than those specified times, a husband and wife should be available to each other and always seek to meet the other's needs.

The Bible offers rich insight into the marriage relationship. I encourage you to spend some time studying what God's Word teaches about your marriage. Knowing and following the Creator's master plan will enrich your marriage—sexually and otherwise.

Prayer: Father God, I want to have a godly intimacy with my husband. Let me see and understand the importance of having such a deep relationship with my man. Clear my spirit to receive this teaching. Amen.

Action:

- Take care to remain attractive on the outside.
- Develop a feminine and serene style to your life.

- Demonstrate your Christian faith through your lifestyle.
- Develop a quiet and gentle spirit that is attractive to your husband.

Because the Lord is my Shepherd,
I have everything I need!
He lets me rest in the meadow grass
and leads me beside the quiet streams.
He gives me new strength.
He helps me do what honors him the most.
Even when walking through the dark valley
   of death
I will not be afraid, for you are close beside me,
guarding, guiding all the way.
You provide delicious food for me
in the presence of my enemies.
You have welcomed me as your guest;
blessings overflow!
Your goodness and unfailing kindness shall
be with me all of my life,
and afterwards I will live with you
forever in your home.

—Psalm 23 tlb

A Gentle, Quiet Spirit

"For I know the plans I have for you," declares
the LORD, "plans to prosper you and not to harm
you, plans to give you hope and a future."
JEREMIAH 29:11

Let me assure you that men love to be in the presence of a real lady. Such a woman makes men feel more masculine, more self-confident, and more relaxed. A real lady influences those around her with these traits instead of just how she looks or dresses—it is about who she is.

What do I mean by a "real lady"? A woman who worked in our local bank for years comes to mind. As she dealt with her customers, she radiated peace. She always offered tranquility, warmth, friendliness, courtesy, and a welcoming spirit. In a woman, these traits can be very feminine, and men respond favorably. The apostle Peter offered this perspective on femininity: "Your adornment must not be merely external...but let it be the hidden person of the heart, with the imperishable quality of a gentle and quiet spirit, which is precious in the sight of God" (1 Peter 3:3-4).

What is feminine? It's not a particular style, form, dress, or interior decorating. Feminine encompasses an infinite variety of physical appearances. It is a softness, gentleness, and graciousness that men don't have. A woman can be the president of a corporation or be a tough and aggressive participant in the business world and still be feminine. To me, feminine also means that a woman has a sense of who she is apart from what she does. She nurtures a strong spirituality and manifests the fruit of the Spirit in every aspect of her life (see Galatians 5:22-23). Femininity also brings to my mind a deep concern for her husband and children, the maternal awareness that she is raising not only her children but generations to follow. A truly feminine woman understands the gift of being a godly wife and mother.

A gentle and quiet spirit, tranquility, being at peace, sharing the fruit of the Spirit with people—these qualities are a direct result of a woman's relationship with God. When a woman is right with God, she doesn't feel any need to prove herself. Confident in herself and aware of her God-given strengths, she doesn't feel compelled to use those strengths to control other people. She enjoys an inner contentment that isn't based on accomplishments, status, authority, power, or other people's opinions.

Prayer: Father God, my heart is heavy in trying to be a woman outside that isn't one on the inside. I truly want that quiet and gentle spirit. Give me the strength to soften my edges. Amen.

Action: Share with a friend who can be trusted how you want to change to be that woman of godly character. Ask her to hold you accountable for those changes.

Put On the New

Now choose life, so that you and your children
may live and that you may love the LORD your
God, listen to his voice, and hold fast to him.

Deuteronomy 30:19

Life is a strange journey, but believe it or not, it isn't as complicated as many of us think. We have two options to choose from—either life or death. It's that basic. Not too much mental power is needed to figure this formula out. When we choose life, we love the Lord and we pay attention to His voice and direction.

> If anyone is in Christ, he is a new creature; the old things
> passed away; behold, new things have come.
> —2 Corinthians 5:17 nasb

What are these old things? They are the natural things that we are born with and the sinful things we need to flee from.

> Put to death the sinful, earthly things lurking within you.
> Have nothing to do with sexual sin, impurity, lust, and
> shameful desires. Don't be greedy, for a greedy person is
> an idolater, worshiping the things of this world. Because

of these sins, the anger of God is coming. You used to do these things when your life was still part of this world. But now is the time to get rid of anger, rage, malicious behavior, slander, and dirty language. Don't lie to each other, for you have stripped off your old sinful nature and all its wicked deeds.

—COLOSSIANS 3:5-9 NLT

These are things we need to put off:

- anger
- rage
- malicious behavior
- slander
- dirty language
- lying

You might ask yourself, "Boy, do I have to give up all of these? What harm is there in keeping a few?" When you choose to keep any one of these, in essence you are choosing death. We must come clean and realize that these will eventually pull us away from God. He has a plan that spells out life and His perfect will for our lives is that we run as fast as we can from these death items. It means we will be choosing new friends, telling different jokes, reading different magazines, holding our tongue when we want to scream in anger. No more gossiping or using foul language. These are all death angels to relationships and particularly our marriage and family.

If not these, what must I put on? What does the new life look like?

Put on your new nature, and be renewed as you learn to know your Creator and become like him. In this new life, it doesn't matter if you are Jew or a Gentile, circumcised or uncircumcised, barbaric, uncivilized, slave or free. Christ is all that matters, and he lives in all of us. Since God chose you to be holy people whom he loves, you must clothe yourselves with tenderhearted mercy, kindness, humility, gentleness, and patience. You must make allowance for each other's faults and forgive anyone who offends you.

Remember, the Lord forgave you, so you must forgive others. Above all, clothe yourselves with love, which binds us all together in perfect harmony.

—Colossians 3:10-14 nlt

What do we need to put on?

- mercy
- kindness
- humility
- gentleness
- patience
- forgiveness
- love

We must be willing to take those things off that lead to death and to put on those things that give life.

Prayer: Father God, give me the courage and strength to take off those things that will prevent me from being all You want me to be. I so want to be the woman after Your own heart. Amen.

Action: Make a list of the things you want to put off. Save some room to list what you're going to do to put them off. Give yourself a deadline for accomplishing each. Then do the same for what you want to put on.

My Lord, Hear Me Now

Be joyful always; pray continually;
give thanks in all circumstances, for this
is God's will for you in Christ Jesus.

1 Thessalonians 5:16-18

God gives us the same love as He gives His Son. And since we are children of God, our prayers can't be denied. Since we abide, He listens! Oh, Lord, how we all want this power and confidence in our prayers. We are not to waver in our faith.

What would our churches and families be like if we knew God in such a powerful way? We long to have the mind of God. He is so much greater than we will and can ever be. We realize there are many barriers to our having this kind of power in our prayers. Daily we must break down and eliminate those hindrances from our daily walks with our Lord.

Each of us have different barriers. Whatever they are, we must be willing to come to grips with them and say, "Hindrances, get thee behind me."

Scripture is so very clear that we are to continually abide in Christ if our prayers are to speedily go to the throne for action. As we arise each day and as we recline each evening after a full day, we are to pray with joy rather than looking on prayer as an irksome duty. As we pray with a pure heart and joy, God adds this to us—you shall ask what you will, and it shall be done to you.

Our goal each day is to get to know our Lord better today than we knew Him yesterday. Make it your priority to spend time with God daily. There's not a single right time or correct place; the only requirement is your willing heart.

Prayer: Father God, You truly are a 24/7 God. Thank You for being there when I need You. Thank You for knowing everything I need or desire before I do. My weaknesses glorify Your mighty strength. Amen.

Action: Really express yourself as a child of God. Draw your heavenly Father a picture or sing to Him without reserve.

Is Not This the Carpenter?

*Isn't this the carpenter? Isn't this Mary's son
and the brother of James, Joseph, Judas and Simon?
Aren't his sisters here with us?*

MARK 6:3

Jesus was not accepted among the people of His hometown. They marveled at the crowds who gathered to hear the wisdom that came from His mouth. However, they were confused. "Isn't this the carpenter?" They thought they knew Jesus too well. They couldn't believe that a simple carpenter could be elevated to the prominence where crowds would gather to hear Him teach.

One man who proclaimed Christ is remembered even today although he took a vow of poverty and lived a simple life. Saint Francis of Assisi died more than 775 years ago, but he has never been forgotten. Great men and women by the hundreds of thousands have lived and died—kings, conquerors, millionaires, artists, musicians, and scholars. All have been forgotten, but not Saint Francis of Assisi. The world stood back in wonder, for Saint Francis had no money, but he acted as if he were richer than the richest. This little man's body was scarred and wracked with pain, yet he sang sweeter than any bird. He was a beggar who smiled as he dined with the famous and laughed as he shared his last crust with a leper. He learned to love everything that lived as part of God's creation.

St. Francis had a secret worth knowing, and the world has been learning it from him ever since. The secret is the wisdom of Jesus, who some thought was just a carpenter. This plain carpenter was a builder of lives. He used more than lumber to create His structures. He used plain ordinary people just like you and me to further God's kingdom. Isn't that amazing?

As we are challenged to be like Jesus, may we, like Francis of Assisi, not let social status or societal limitations prevent us from becoming the person Christ wants us to become.

Prayer: Father God, I, too, can be more than an ordinary carpenter. Light my path so I won't stumble along the way. Your light overcomes darkness and gives me hope for tomorrow. Help me share Your illumination. Amen.

Action: Pray about your potential. Try to see yourself and your life through God's eyes. Ask God how He wants to use you. And be open to the answer!

In Everything, Not For Everything

In everything give thanks; for this is
the will of God in Christ Jesus for you.
1 THESSALONIANS 5:18 NKJV

One evening we received two telephone calls that really test this verse. One was regarding a 15-year-old boy who had just been hospitalized to begin a grueling chemotherapy regimen to combat his newly diagnosed cancer.

The next call was regarding a mother who went in for a midlife hysterectomy. The doctors, in performing a routine biopsy, discovered cervical cancer.

How do we say "Thank You God" for tragedies and sudden crises that threaten to destroy our world? I struggled with this question until I realized that this passage says, "in everything," not "for everything."

"In everything" is not the same as "for everything." We don't give thanks for evil or for its tragic results. And at some time or another, we all come face to face with evil or an unexpected crisis that threatens us or our family. At such times, no mother can be thankful for the evil that threatens her loved ones, but she can and must be thankful to the God who oversees all that comes our way.

Even in the midst of our pain, God is always at work. We can remain grateful throughout our ordeal because we live in Jesus Christ and because we know that God cares for us even more than we care for our own children. God is the only perfect parent—and in Him, we find refuge in the day of trouble. Through every circumstance that comes our way, God continues to transform us into the image of His Son.

Matthew Henry, the well-known Bible commentator, made the following entry in his diary after he had been robbed:

"Let me be thankful—first, because I was never robbed before; second, because although they took my wallet, they did not take my life; third, because although they took my all, it was not much; and fourth, because it was I who was robbed, not I who robbed."

Here is a man who knew how to make lemonade out of a lemon. Here is a man who could give thanks in everything.

The art of successful living is to seek out thankfulness in all of life's events—to see meaning in every challenge and trust that God will work every adversity to our ultimate good.

It's like the mom who opened the door to her young son's bedroom and saw the boy digging in a large pile of manure. The mother asked, "What on earth are you doing?"

Without a pause the boy replied, "Mommy, with all this manure there's got to be a pony in here somewhere!"

Prayer: Father God, may Your will be done in my life. Today and every day. Help me give thanks "in everything." Help me to look closely to see the good in all that You do. Amen.

Action: Give thanks for your trial and praises for the way God is shaping your life through all circumstances.

Trust Him for Everything

But I trust in You, O LORD; I say,
"You are my God." My times are in Your hands.
PSALM 31:14-15

Why are some people healed and others not? Why do some get miracles while others pray just as hard and every bit as sincerely but remain ill, or even die from disease? After endless months and years of petitioning God, I've come to realize that "God's will" be done.

And His will is good!

He has a perfect plan and timetable for each of us. The sooner we recognize this in our Christian walks the quicker we'll understand that His thoughts and His ways are greater than our ways.

Yes, God healed me of my mantle cell lymphoma, and I give Him praise for that. From the very beginning I claimed John 11:4 as my theme verse:

> This sickness is not to end in death, but for the glory of
> God, so that the Son of God may be glorified by it.

What amazing peace I received when I turned this dramatic situation over to God. Bob and I agreed that through this valley God was going to be glorified. That declaration grew out of years and years of previous prayers and diligent study of God's Word and His promises. We came to understand—and prove—that we could trust God for everything. Yes, even for our very lives.

No matter how circumstances appeared on the surface, we were convinced God was working out all things for His glory and our personal interest. This kind of faith makes life so exciting. We don't have to search the world for the purpose of life; we've found it and live it daily. The Westminster Confession of Faith expresses our goal very clearly: Man's chief end is to glorify God and enjoy Him forever.

Prayer helps us establish this purpose in a profound and deeply personal way. Without the wondrous gift of prayer, how could we ever gain the sense that our lives on earth have meaning?

We couldn't. We would be in that last and desolate state described by the apostle Paul—"without hope and without God in the world" (Ephesians 2:12).

We essentially have two choices. We can pray, or we can lose heart (Luke 18:1). You and I can live lives marked by faith and hope, or we can surrender to lives filled with fear, anxiety, worry, and despair. Give praise to God because we have His strong arms around us! We cry out to Him because—in Jesus—He calls out to us. When life seems overwhelming, God wants us to lift our hands to Him as His little children, wanting to be held in His loving arms. We may not even know what's wrong or why we feel heavy-hearted or afraid. And we don't have to know. All we really need to know is where to turn.

When we face the many pressures of life there is only one effective successful way "through it all"—we are to pray. Prayer is our way to the place of power, our path to the solutions for life's indecipherable dilemmas. Unbearable pressures need not be withstood by us when God's strong and willing shoulders are ready to bear them:

"Cast all your anxiety on him because he cares for you" (1 Peter 5:7).

Prayer: Father God, let me lean and trust Your promises for my life. You are the same in the past, present, and future. You never change. Amen.

Action: Cast one of your cares upon God. Remember, God's clock is different than our watch.

A Safe Refuge—Home

God is our refuge and strength, an ever-present help in trouble.
Therefore we will not fear, though the earth give way and
the mountains fall into the heart of the sea, though its waters
roar and foam and the mountains quake with their surging.

PSALM 46:1-3

God is a refuge in times of trouble, tumult, and turmoil. "When the ground starts shifting under my feet," the psalmist is saying, "when my world becomes a worrisome, fearful place, I take refuge in my God."

God is a refuge for His people. He always has been, and He always will be. And I believe that a godly home—a home where Jesus Christ is obeyed and honored—becomes a physical refuge, a place where people worn down by the noise, commotion, and hostility of the outside world can find a safe resting place. A welcoming home is a place you and others enjoy coming to.

If you live in a house with small children, you may already be shaking your head. "What do you mean by 'noise, commotion, and hostility of the outside world'? I have to leave home to get away from the turmoil!" Believe me, I understand. But even in the rough-and-tumble of family living, home can be a safe haven and even a place of quiet (at least some of the time). If you find noise and activity crowding your family life and pushing and pulling at you, making the extra effort to create a sense of refuge in the midst of it can pay wonderful dividends.

Maybe this concept depends on how you define "refuge." I'm not talking about a hole you disappear down to eat and sleep and then emerge from to go about the business of life. A welcoming home is where real life happens. It's where personalities are nurtured, growth is stimulated, and people feel free to be and improve themselves. That caring, nurturing quality—not the absence of noise or occasional strife—is what makes a home a refuge.[1]

As women, we are the thermostat of our home. We are the ones who make it happen. God has built into us that desire to build a refuge and nest for our husband and children. If it's going to happen, it will happen because of us. A woman is fortunate if she is blessed with a husband who lends a hand to make it happen. Your heartbeat for your home will be the driving force behind making it happen.

Don't have any great expectations about anyone else helping you out in this project. Don't expect it to be done overnight—it's a lifetime project. Do it because you have been called to make that cozy nest for your loved ones. Besides, you also receive a great benefit from having a cozy, charming refuge.

> By wisdom a house is built, and through understanding it
> is established; through knowledge its rooms are filled with
> rare and beautiful riches.
>
> —Proverbs 24:3-4

Prayer: Father God, let me with passion build the refuge for my family. Let me see the long-term rewards for me and my family. Amen.

Action: Take a survey of your home and figure out a game plan for developing your home into a godly refuge.

A Look at Anger

Good sense makes a man [woman] restrain his
[her] anger, and it is his glory to overlook a
transgression or an offense.

Proverbs 19:11 AMP

Anger burns like a hot brushfire. As I read my daily newspapers and view the TV news, I am constantly reminded of the sin of anger. Not a day goes by when the media doesn't report the sad results of anger: murder, road rage, drunk driving, drive-by assaults, arson fires, child beating, rape, and so on.

A healthy relationship cannot exist where anger exists. The two do not go together. In order for healthy relationships and friendships to flourish we must be able to control this raging fire that exists in many human beings. The book of Proverbs gives some insight concerning the subject of anger.

These passages are from The Living Bible:

- "A short-tempered man is a fool. He hates the man who is patient" (14:17).
- "A quick-tempered man starts fights; a cool-tempered man tries to stop them" (15:18).

- "It is better to be slow-tempered than famous; it is better to have self-control than to control an army" (16:32).

- "A fool gets into constant fights. His mouth is his undoing! His words endanger him" (18:6-7).

- "A short-tempered man must bear his own penalty; you can't do much to help him. If you try once you must try a dozen times" (19:19).

- "Keep away from angry, short-tempered men, lest you learn to be like them and endanger your soul" (22:24-25).

- "A rebel shouts in anger; a wise man holds his temper in and cools it" (29:11).

- "There is more hope for a fool than for a man of quick temper" (29:20).

- "A hot-tempered man starts fights and gets into all kinds of trouble" (29:22).

If anger is one of your enemies, go to God in prayer and ask for healing. Anger is a cancer that can destroy your body if not addressed. Don't wait until it is too late. Healthy relationships demand that anger be conquered.

Prayer: Father God, help me examine myself to see if there is any evidence of anger in my life. If so, I want to give it to You. Amen.

Action: Release your anger and discover ways to change behaviors even as God changes your heart and character.

Christ be my light
  to illumine and guide me!
Christ be my shield
  to cover and guard me!
Christ be under me, Christ be over me,
  Christ beside me, left and right!
Christ before me,
  behind me, about me—
Christ this day,
  within, without me!
Christ in every heart
  that thinks of me—
Christ in every mouth
  that speaks to me!
Christ in every eye that sees me—
  Christ in every ear
    that hears me!
  —FROM THE BREASTPLATE OF ST. PATRICK

The Lost Mitt

And the LORD will continually guide you, and satisfy your
desire in scorched places, and give strength to your bones; and
you will be like…a spring of water whose waters do not fail.
ISAIAH 58:11 NASB

It was my son Brad's first real leather baseball mitt. Bob had taught him how to break it in with special oil to form the pocket just right for catching the ball. The oil was rubbed into the pocket. Then Brad tossed his baseball from hand to hand to form a pocket just right for him. Brad loved his mitt and worked for hours each day to make it fit just right. He was so happy to have such a special glove for his games and practices.

One afternoon after practice one of the older boys asked to see Brad's mitt. He looked it over, then tossed it away into the grassy field. Brad ran to find his special possession, but he couldn't find it. Nowhere was his mitt to be found. With a frightened, hurt heart, Brad came home in tears.

I encouraged him by saying that the mitt is there someplace and let's go look. "But Mom, I did search the lot, and it's not there," replied Brad, in tears.

So I said, "Brad, let's pray and ask God to help us." By now it was

107

beginning to get dark and we needed to hurry, so we jumped into the car. As I drove to the baseball field, we asked God to please guide our steps directly to the exact spot where the glove was. After parking, we quickly headed for the field. Again we asked God to point us in the right direction. Brad ran into the tall grass and, about 20 feet away, was Brad's glove.

God answers our prayers. Sometimes it's "wait," "yes," or "later." For Brad that day it was a yes. God said in essence, "I'll direct you to find the mitt of this young boy whose heart was broken because of a bully and a lost glove."

Do you have a "lost glove" today? Go before God and praise Him for the promise He gave us in Isaiah 58:11. If God says it, believe it. He will direct you and guide you. Open your heart to listen to what His direction is, then press ahead. The grass may seem too tall for you to see very far, but trust the Lord and keep walking until you feel in your heart the peace you desire. God may lead in a direction you least expect, but step forward with confidence in the Lord.

Prayer: Lord, what an encouragement to me that You care about the smallest details of my life. I do want to be a spring of water to those around me. Amen.

Action: Recognize something very simple that has weighed on your heart for a long time. It isn't small now, is it? Pray about these things and watch for God's direction.

*C*elebrate Each Day

Teach us to number our days and recognize how few
they are; help us to spend them as we should.
PSALM 90:12 TLB

*H*ow often do we talk in terms of days? Usually our reference is in terms of years. She's 37 years old, they were married 15 years ago, I've been sober for 10 years, and World War II was 68 years ago.

One thing about youth is that they think they have nine lives and they will never get old. They think they are "eternally young"! But as we get older, we realize that we are running out of years, and our thoughts turn to months and to days.

Today's verse suggests that we are to number our days. We are encouraged to live each day to the fullest so that when our lives draw to an end, we have gained a "heart of wisdom" or spent each day as we should. When we live each day unto the Lord, we live it with gusto and enthusiasm for Him.

I have found that as I get older, the inevitables of life happen, and I must learn to adjust to the unknowns that appear from time to time. One cannot do this in terms of years but only from day-to-day and often from hour-to-hour. Aging isn't a choice—it just happens and it isn't always the "Golden Years"—they don't have as much gold as we thought.

With each new pain and ache, don't become negative, but rather celebrate the life that God has given you. How we respond to these aches will determine how we grow old.

Prayer: Father God, let me enjoy each day as if it were my last day. Let my eyes see Your beauty of nature and my nose smell the fragrance of Your flowers. Each day is all I have. Amen.

Action: Do what you would do if you only had one day to live. Share it with a friend.

Have the Right Perspective

You are my refuge and my shield;
your word is my source of hope.
PSALM 119:114 NLT

People have asked me how I can be so upbeat when so many things around me are negative. I guess it's because of my perspective on life. Through Scripture and life experiences, I have come to trust that God has a master plan for my life. He knew me from the beginning of time. He knows my beginning, and He knows the end. He is the Alpha and the Omega. I've learned that He has taken care of me in the past, He is taking care of me in the present, thus I have assurance that He will take care of my future. A long time ago I told God, "Thy will be done in my life."

His words give me so much comfort. I have learned that I can count on His promises. When I face troubles that seem insurmountable, I have a hope that is powerful and limitless. My hope in the Lord is absolute. When the psalmist tells me that God is my shield and that His promises and His Word are my only source of hope, I believe it. God's character is one of honor, trust, and reliability that I can bank on for my well-being.

God's Word brings me light on a foggy day, it brings me hope when

I become discouraged, and it helps me not to make a mountain out of a molehill. His Word gives me the right perspective on life. I know my time on earth is such a short time and my time with Him after this earthly experience will be for eternity.

> Teach us to make the most of our time, so that we may grow in wisdom.
>
> —PSALM 90:12

Prayer:　Father God, thanks for sharing with me Your wisdom, so that I have hope for the future. Your Word gives me hope for that future. When others fret and worry, You have given me an eternal perspective. Amen.

Action:　Search Scripture to find a promise that you can put your faith in. Claim it as your theme verse for life.

A Gift of Tea

*Always seek after that which is good for
one another and for all people.*
1 THESSALONIANS 5:15 NASB

What better gift can you give someone than a little bit of relaxation and peace of mind in today's hectic and busy world? I believe that tea provides that perfect respite for anyone. I am becoming more of a tea person each day I live. I love the beauty and simplicity of tea time.

> What a great time this is to be alive. The possibilities for us in Christ are limitless. For every opportunity that He brings to us may our hearts say "yes"—to His plan, His grace, and His glory.
>
> —ROY LESSIN

One of the nicest things about discovering the beauty of tea is that I have my Bob to enjoy a steaming cup of tea with me. Since he enjoys having a pot of tea in the afternoon, I've been able to delight in this great retirement adventure.

Tea is a great gift idea for anyone of any age. Tea's popularity makes it easy to find gifts in all sizes and price ranges—from tea cups or teapots to scone mixes and lovely teas of different origins and flavors.

Tea makes a lovely hostess gift and the recipient is touched by your thoughtfulness.

After one of those days that seems to go on forever, take a break, sit back, take just a little bit of time for yourself and relax with a delicious cup of tea. Hot or iced, you will discover that there is a way to experience comfort and serenity wherever you are.

In a fast moving world we must take time to refresh ourselves. Nothing works better than a short break from your daily routine to stop, sip, and be still.

Prayer: Father God, thanks for reminding me that I need to take a break from the routines of the day and refresh myself with a break called tea. Amen.

Action: Take a moment, heat up a pot of water, pick out your favorite cup and saucer, dip a teabag in the cup, pour hot water over the teabag, let it settle for a minute, add a drop of honey and a splash of milk—sit back and enjoy the pause that refreshes.

Make Time for a Garden

The lesson I have thoroughly learnt,
and wish to pass on to others, is to know the
enduring happiness that the love of a garden gives...

GERTRUDE JEKYLL

Spending time in nature is a way to experience the awesome sanctuary of the Lord. You can take in the beauty of buds and blooms, sprigs of green and dangling clusters of purple. You can breathe in deeply and allow the scent of lilacs, roses, or mint to fill you with delight. Step outside of your yard or garden and the wonders just keep on coming. The fragrance of sweet peas and clematis might cover you as you walk around your neighborhood or at a local park.

Creation reminds us of God's precious, attentive care to each and every living thing. It beckons us to fill our hearts with joy and to rid our minds of worries and complaints. There is refreshment for body, mind, and spirit when you take time to be outdoors and in God's playground.

How could such sweet and wholesome hours be reckoned
but in herbs and flowers?

—ANDREW MARVELL

I find that I want to rejoice after a short time in the sunlight or in the presence of a majestic tree that reaches toward heaven. The fresh air makes my heart soar as I think of so many ways that God's miracles touch my life. Those miracles are all around you and me. We just have to be willing and fortunate enough to notice them and be grateful.

Take time to walk with God in your garden, beside a rushing river, along a wooded trail. You will meet God on this adventure and experience sweet communion with the Maker of such wondrous life.

Prayer:　Father God, let me learn to slow down from my hectic pace of life. I so enjoy being around all of Your creations of nature. Give me the time to develop greenery in and around my home. Amen.

Action:　Go out and bring back a beautiful bouquet of your favorite flower. Have them displayed so your family can also admire and appreciate them.

Be a Woman of Character

Be beautiful inside, in your hearts, with the lasting charm
of a gentle and quiet spirit which is so precious to God.
1 Peter 3:4 TLB

In America, consumers spend billions of dollars each year to make themselves look younger and to push back the aging process. Men and women spend a lot of money to make themselves more attractive. Yes, even men are buying cosmetics and having plastic surgery. When I go by the cosmetic counter at my favorite department store, the ladies gather around the beauty consultant as if they were at McDonald's waiting in line for a hamburger, fries, and drink.

Even in economic downturns, people continue to buy cosmetics. We all want to be beautiful on the outside. Improving our outward beauty is one thing; improving our inward beauty is far more difficult and more important.

Even though we are going through difficult economic days, we can still radiate our inner beauty. Don't slide into the rut of being an ugly complainer. We can still be charming even in very tough times.

I have the privilege of knowing some very godly women who model their inward beauty to me. They are wonderful ladies to be around. They adorn themselves with a gentle and quiet spirit which is pleasing to the Lord. As I grow older, I want to be more lovely inside, keeping in mind that growing older brings me closer to my Lord.

All of the commercial ads that we see in the media will not stop the aging process nor bring back our youth, but God does promise in Isaiah 40:30-31 a formula that gives us renewed strength:

> Even youths grow tired and weary, and the young men stumble and fall, but those who hope in the LORD will renew their strength; they will soar on wings like eagles, they will run and not grow weary, they will walk and not faint.

This is definitely a promise of spiritual vitality that defies the ravages of time. When we look to Scripture we can develop into the kind of woman that God created us to be—a woman of character. His promises come alive when we put our trust in Him for strength of heart, energy for our soul, and a vigor for our spirit.

Prayer: Father God, keep me from concentrating on the outward part of my life and let me develop the muscles of my inside person. Put blinders on my eyes when I view all the ads that suggest that the outward appearance makes a successful woman. Amen.

Action: Concentrate on the inside beauty today.

The Strength of Women

In quietness and trust is your strength.
ISAIAH 30:15

A proper lady may be gentle and tender, but she is far from being weak. Filling our lives with loveliness takes physical stamina, emotional strength, and spiritual courage. And that's no modern feminist secret. Beautiful women of all ages have shaped the world with the power of their femininity.

I think of Queen Esther standing in her inner court of the palace, resplendent in her royal robes, risking her life to save her people. Or that admirable woman of Proverbs 31 running a household and a business while still finding time for volunteer work. Or my own sweet mother, who ran a little dress shop to support us after my father died, and who taught me to love beauty and reach out to love other people.

Or what about Sarah Edwards, the wife of the famous theologian Jonathan Edwards? In the early to mid 1700s, with no modern conveniences, she ran a household and raised eleven children. She made all the family's clothes, cooked and prepared all the foods, worked the garden, made candles, and stoked the fire. Many guests filled their busy colonial home. She taught her children to work hard, to respect others, and to show good manners. And she surrounded all her teaching with her love for God and each child.

> It is the glow within that creates beauty. People are like stained-glass windows. They sparkle like crystal in the sun. At night they continue to sparkle only if there is light from within.
>
> —Bonnie Green

All of this time, hard work, and love showed up in the children's accomplishments and attitudes. Her children passed on this same love and discipline to their children.

Timothy Dwight, Sarah's grandson and former president of Yale University, said, "All that I am and all I will be I owe to my mother."

Strong ladylike qualities is part of our heritage as women. When we make the effort to cultivate such gentle strength, we cannot only enrich our own lives and make life a little better for those we encounter, we also pass on the spirit of being a lady to the next generation.[2]

> Do not be stingy with your heart.
>
> —Joseph Fort Newton

Prayer: Father God, give me the added strength to be a strong wife and mom. Teach me how to hang in with my husband and children when I feel like giving up. Amen.

Action: Hang in when you feel like giving up.

God Is a Redeemer

I will repay you for the years that the locusts have eaten.
JOEL 2:25

Each community has its tragic stories that have a longtime effect on their area. Such was the case last year for one Orange County community in Southern California. It started out as a normal day, a family had breakfast, each member went about their normal routine. The mother, her mother, and her three young children were stopped in the slow lane on our I-5 freeway in Mission Viejo. In an instant their lives were changed forever. A big-rig truck loaded with electronics struck the family's minivan from the rear. All three of the young children were killed.

This news was felt by our whole community. Parents reached out in utter sorrow, the news media stayed with the story for weeks. It made all of us realize again what is so important in this crazy world we live in. Their local pastor stated, "It was just this freak accident that caught us off guard and shook our world. In the midst of this it clarified things that are important, like family, creating a future, and the delightful memory of three wonderful children."

A year later we find the parents working with the Truck Safety Coalition to help make changes in the trucking industry to bring greater safety and accountability to their members. They want their crusade for truck safety to go national. They want strict regulation of trucking companies and their drivers. They want federal monitoring of truck driving records.

One of their neighbors expressed what they have all learned from this tragic event: "I've learned how a moment can change everything and how we can't take a day for granted, and that it's been a lesson in faith. It's given us an opportunity to teach our children about eternity so we can lead our lives."

The Scripture passage for today—"I will repay you for the years that the locusts have eaten"—has come true for this family. In this weekend's local paper it was announced that this couple gave birth to a set of triplets, one year from the date when the locust took their three young children away from them. God is truly a redeemer. What man intended for evil—God meant for good.

God is good—all the time!

Prayer: Father God, thank You for showing me in real life that you do redeem what the locusts have eaten. Let me trust You more in my everyday walk with you. Amen.

Action: Claim God's promise that He is a redeemer.

Five Ways to Deepen Your Friendship

*Love is very patient and kind, never jealous
or envious, never boastful or proud.*

1 CORINTHIANS 13:4 TLB

For whatever reasons, it's often not as easy for a man to cultivate a friendship as it is for a woman. Furthermore, if your husband doesn't come from a very demonstrative family, he may not have a good male role model for how to be a friend to his male friends or even to you. You may have to teach him how to be a friend. Following are five points that may help you:

1. Assign top priority to your friendship. How important are your friendships? How you spend your time will show you! Each of us does what we want to; nothing gets in the way of doing what is most important to us. So consider again how important your friendships are to you. Make room and take time to develop good friends.

2. Cultivate transparency in your relationships. When we are honest with ourselves about who we are (emotionally and otherwise), we can be a better friend. Our willingness to be open about who we are encourages trust and

openness on the part of the other person. Be yourself in your openness. Just remember that what is shared in private stays in private.

3. Dare to risk talking about your affection. When building that friendship with your husband, take a risk and show and share your affection to your mate. One expression that Bob shares with me when he does some kind deed or gives me a hug is this saying: "Just another way to show that I love you!" Be willing to be open in your conversation about your affection for each other. Tell your mate what makes you feel good—it's okay to be shy and bashful and even to get embarrassed—but do it anyway.

4. Give your mate freedom. Love is never oppressive or possessive. Let your mate be all that God wants them to be. That means in failure as well as in success. Your mate needs to be free from words that discourage and words that harm. Be a part of your friends' dreams. Help give wings to their plans for the future. A friend is one who gives encouragement and is not a giver of a wet blanket. Give your friend the freedom to be themselves. Encourage your friend to be the unique person God created them to be.

5. Learn the language of love. Each of us needs to learn how to say, "I love you." I'm not talking about only speaking out loud these three powerful words (although that's an important thing to do). We need to also say "I love you" through our respect.

Certain rituals and traditions in our family also enable us to express our love for one another. We kiss each other goodnight and say, "May God bless your sleep." We celebrate our love on anniversaries and birthdays by giving each other small gifts. We telephone one another when we're apart, visit one of our favorite restaurants on special occasions, etc. All of these things—spontaneous acts as well as carefully planned events—make for a special friendship.

Prayer: Father God, let me broaden my friendship to my husband by considering these five guidelines for friendship. Amen.

Action: For the next five weeks take one of the above to work on to strengthen your friendship with your husband.

Check Your Power Source

The Lord says, "I will make my people strong with power from me!...Wherever they go they will be under my personal care."
ZECHARIAH 10:12 TLB

The other morning while preparing breakfast, I put two pieces of bread in the toaster, pushed down the lever, walked away to soft-boil my eggs, to return in a few minutes to find my bread still in the toaster—but not toasted. I scratched my head, pushed down the lever once again, but this time I didn't walk away. I stayed close by to observe what went wrong the first time. Again no toast and no hot wires visible to toast my bread. "Why, oh why," I asked, "why isn't my bread toasting?"

Over my shoulder my Bob uttered, "Have you ever thought of plugging the cord into the socket?" Dumb is me! Why would I expect toast when the toaster wasn't plugged into the power source for the toaster? Later that morning I reflected on that situation at breakfast and thought of why I don't get answers from God when I'm not plugged into Him.

In Southern California where I live, we have many service companies that want to take care of my every need. We have personal trainers, personal shoppers, home decorators, personal animal groomers, valet parking, and personal guides for our amusement parks. However, none of these services can take care of our spiritual needs. We need something much larger in life than a service provides.

Since God has promised to make us strong with His power source, we need to break out and take some control over our lives. God has given us many truths that enable us to make appropriate choices for proper and healthy living.

When we are confronted with certain illnesses, as I have been and so have many of you, we must rely on good common sense. Your intuition will give you insight on what needs to be done. Just make sure you are plugged in to the right power source.

Remember that God is always there looking over your shoulder. When He is needed, He is there! You are under His personal care at all times.

Prayer: Father God, let me rely on Your power more. The weight that I'm personally carrying is too heavy. Help me to say "no" when I find myself trying to solve all my problems. Amen.

Action: Go to God in prayer for your decisions. Depend upon Him more each day. Step down so He can step up.

Hurry, Hurry, Hurry

Man is never so tall as when he kneels before God—
never so great as when he humbles himself before God.
And the man who kneels to God can stand up to anything.

Louis H. Evans

Faster, faster, faster.

I'm always on the go, and you probably are too. Technology, marvelous as it may be, hasn't done a thing to ease our pace. In fact, it has pushed us harder and faster. The faster I move, the more someone wants and expects me to take it up yet another notch. I'm certain this is not what God had in mind when He created us. As His children we need to fight the urge to be swept along in this hurry-up mentality.

So what's the alternative? Becoming castaways on a tropical island? Getting rid of our computers and cell phones? No, if we're to function effectively, we must find a healthy balance. Living in hyperdrive may not be God's will, but neither is checking out of life and collecting cobwebs. I remember something Chuck Swindoll said years ago: "The zealot says, 'I would rather burn out than rust out!' But what's the difference? Either way you're out!"

Again, there must be balance, a moderation (my family's favorite word). In order to accomplish this equilibrium I've learned to pray on my feet or—to say it another way—to pray on the go.

From one end to the other, Scripture gives us examples of where and how to pray:

- "Pray without ceasing" (1 Thessalonians 5:17 NKJV).
- "Call upon Me in the day of trouble; I shall rescue you" (Psalm 50:15 NASB).
- "Pour out your heart before Him; God is a refuge for us" (Psalm 62:8 NASB).
- "Seek the LORD while He may be found; call upon Him while He is near" (Isaiah 55:6 NASB).
- "Ask, and it will be given to you; seek, and you will find; knock, and it will be opened to you" (Matthew 7:7 NASB).

One of the main purposes of faith is to bring us into direct, personal, vital contact with the living God. When we pray, we admit our profound need, our helplessness to do life without Him. Even though God knows all of our daily needs, our praying for them changes our attitude from complaints and criticism to praise. In some real-but-mysterious way, praying allows us to participate in God's personal plan for our lives.

Jesus taught His disciples that "at all times they ought to pray and not lose heart" (Luke 18:1). Even though answers to prayer don't always come along immediately, we should not be discouraged...or stop praying! Oh, how my family had to learn these things as we prayed fervently for God to heal my cancer and all that goes with being a cancer patient. We wanted an immediate healing that would have the medical profession declaring, "It's a miracle!" Instead we had to learn time and again that God's timetable was not our own.[3]

Prayer: Father God, let me slow down and let me spend more time in Your presence. I know that prayer gives me strength to get through the day. Amen.

Action: Start today to spend time with God.

Be a Sower of Seeds

Yes, I am the Vine; you are the branches.
Whoever lives in me and I in him
shall produce a large crop of fruit.
For apart from me you can't do a thing.

JOHN 15:5 TLB

My husband, Bob, comes from a line of Texas farmers. He seems to have a green thumb in whatever he plants. Early in our marriage it was evident that our landscaping was the best in the neighborhood. The lawns were the greenest and the flowers the brightest. He has always told me you have to have three elements to have things grow: sun, water, and fertilizer. With those three you can grow any plant well.

A smart woman once told me that a wise person does in her youth what a foolish person does in her old age. Let's not wait until we are old to do what we should have done when we were young.

It is a well-known biblical principle: Whatever we sow, we reap. The harvest always comes after the planting. All other things being equal, we can anticipate that with good weather and adequate rain, we will have a large crop—if we have made the effort to sow in the first place. In a sense, I am experiencing a harvest time in my life right now. I am reaping the results of friendship seeds sown in other seasons. I remember busy times when I almost didn't have time for friends—when a phone call, or a note, or a luncheon date, or even a word of prayer was truly a sacrifice of my time, when making time for others was truly a struggle.

How glad I am that I made those efforts to sow seeds of friendship and love and to cultivate those crops carefully. Now I have the privilege of reaping an abundant harvest. I am so blessed to have all my family, friends, and loved ones around me during this time of life.

To everything there is a season, but know what season you are in. Dream big and sow big! But try not to let ambition turn your joy into drudgery. You reap what you sow, but there will be surprises.

> This is to my Father's glory, that you bear much fruit, showing yourselves to be my disciples.
>
> —John 15:8

Prayer: Father God, help me today to keep my heart and mind focused on You. Your goodness and blessing in my life have enriched my faith beyond my own belief. Thank You! Amen.

Action: Go to your local nursery, pick out a few packets of seeds, and plant them at home.

God Is Bound by His Promises

Keep watching and praying, that you may not enter into temptation; the spirit is willing, but the flesh is weak.

MATTHEW 26:41

God always keeps His promises. His character will not let Him fall back. In truth, all prayers offered through His Son, Jesus, are bound to be heard. God finds joy in keeping His promises.

God's actions are always consistent with His character, including His love, righteousness, holiness, and justice. He cannot lay aside any one of His attributes and act independently of it. It is part of His being to be just. In all of His actions, God acts with fairness. If He did less, He would no longer be God!

> The Rock! His work is perfect, for all His ways are just; a God of faithfulness and without injustice, righteous and upright is He.
>
> —DEUTERONOMY 32:4 NASB

We live in a day where all aspects of life are being undermined by dishonesty. Families have lost much of their retirement funds because they believed executives' promises that were made with their fingers crossed behind their backs.

Oh, how desperate our country is for people with character! We look to our sports heroes, our political leaders, our corporate leadership, the stars of movies and television, and even our spiritual leaders, hoping they will show us how people of character live. Each time we feel comfortable that a certain personality has the answer, we are disappointed by some revelation of broken dreams and promises.

We expect people to do what they say they are going to do. We are disappointed when plumbers, electricians, painters, or coworkers can't do what they've said they are going to do. They miss the appointment or don't deliver their product on time—and here we patiently wait and nothing happens. Even parents tell their children that such-and-such will happen on Saturday, and it doesn't happen as promised. How many children go to their rooms to cry because a promise was broken?

We are so thankful we have One who never goes back on His promises. God always keeps His word. If He said it, you can believe it. Let's all learn from the Master of character to "just do what you say you are going to do."

Prayer: Father God, thanks for being a promise-keeper. You are the model for every woman who wants to be an honorable woman. You give great confidence from Your Word because I know You won't break Your promise. If You said it, I believe it. Amen.

Action: Make and keep a promise to someone today—even a small one. Make this practice a discipline of your faith.

How Is Your Heart?

O God, my heart is quiet and confident. No
wonder I can sing your praises!
PSALM 57:7 TLB

A quiet and confident heart sounds so lovely, doesn't it? This kind of heart gives us stability in a life that's constantly saying, "Faster, faster, hurry, hurry!" Few of us have this kind of heart. One of our pleas is, "How do I find the time?"

One way to get started is to make morning devotion time a priority for your life. Put it on your daily planner (the same as for any appointment) and have your spouse hold you accountable for this commitment. Morning is a great time to meet God because it gives you a great start for the day. Some of us are morning people and some are late-evening people. You decide what is the best time for you.

Psalm 5:3 gives us motivation to meet God: "In the morning, O LORD, You will hear my voice; in the morning I will order my prayer to You and eagerly watch" (NASB). What kind of structure might you have? Here's a suggestion:

1. Pray for guidance so that you focus and dedicate this time just for the two of you (see Psalm 148:1-5).

2. Read a portion of Scripture. If you are new to the faith you
   might begin with the book of John (see Psalm 119:18).

3. Have a time for prayer. You might want to use the word
   "ACTS" to remember what four areas to include:

   • A—Adoration. This segment is all about God. You
     love Him, you adore Him, you thank Him for all
     He's done for you. Reflect on who He is (read Lam-
     entations 3:22-23).

   • C—Confession. You agree with God on what sins
     you have committed. You need to come to God with
     a clean heart (read Psalm 66:18).

   • T—Thanksgiving. Be specific in thanking God for
     all He has given you. Thank Him for your marriage,
     your family, your home, your pastor, your job, and so
     on. Even thank Him for your difficult times—after
     all, these are events that create growth in your life
     (read 1 Thessalonians 5:18).

   • S—Supplication. Make your requests known to God.
     Remember to include requests for others, such as gov-
     ernment officials, missionaries, students, and believers
     in other countries (read Matthew 7:7).

Become a member of the morning watch. There are no member-
ship forms to fill out or any monthly dues. It takes 21 days to start a
new habit. Begin today and see how it will have a positive influence
on the rest of the day—and transform your life.

Prayer: Father God, I want to meet You the first thing in the morning. When the alarm goes off, let me jump out of bed and be on time for our appointment. Amen.

Action: Start forming your new habit tomorrow morning. Remember, it only takes 21 days to form a new habit.

Joy Comes in the Morning

Weeping may go on all night,
but in the morning there is joy.
PSALM 30:5 TLB

Tears, for me, have been so cleansing. My pillow was soaked sometimes by all my discouragement during the cancer ordeal. While you are on this journey, tears help you to be transparent to yourself, your mate, your family, and the world. My Bob has been so great during this journey. At times, the caregiver has a tougher time than the patient. When I get weepy, Bob is always there to soothe and comfort me. He knows I don't need any answers from him, just support.

It's okay to cry—don't try to hide it. Be real; your illness, trial, or loss is real. The people around you need to know that you feel the pain deeply. That's one of the blessings of a difficulty that is too great to hide, it forces us to be vulnerable with the people around us. Struggles take away all the phoniness of life, and you gain a new understanding of how precious a new day is to be real with yourself and with others. The things you used to think were important aren't nearly as important as they used to be. Life is viewed with a whole new perspective.

Do you know what the other blessing is? The more real you are with others, the more genuine they will be in their responses to you and your trial. If you've spent years keeping people at a safe distance because you were afraid to reveal your weaknesses or your worries, trust God to shape those relationships into more meaningful connections. You will learn how freeing and life-changing it can be to embrace the joy of honesty. Be open during your conversations with dear friends and family members. Children, depending on their ages, don't always need to know everything; however, they need to be aware that life is difficult for you at the moment. This knowledge gives them opportunities to learn compassion.

After each cry, the new day reflects the joy of Jesus. His promises and His love will be made more real to you.

Prayer: Father God, let me be brave even when tears flow from my heart. Let me know that it's okay to cry. Please give me joy in the morning. Amen.

Action: Look for that joy in the morning. And when you discover it, pass it along to your family, to friends, and to strangers you encounter throughout the day. Watch the joy multiply!

If I Could Do It Again

There is an appointed time for everything.
And there is a time for every event under heaven.

ECCLESIASTES 3:1 NASB

Repeating something from the past so that you can do it better, more perfectly, or more lovingly is a nice thought, but none of us are granted do-overs in this life. We can wish all we want, but we can't do it all again. As deeply as I might like to go back to certain seasons of my life or revisit certain attitudes or decisions I made in my younger years…I can't do it. No one can. God has placed each one of our lives on a timeline, with a specific beginning and a specific end. And wherever we may be on that line, going forward is our only option. We've looked at this verse before, but let's revisit it…one good thing about studying the Bible is that we can go back to verses over and over. And our lives will be better off for such returns! This verse is encouraging and comforting, especially when we are tempted to revisit the past or to spend long stretches of time dwelling on our mistakes:

> "For I know the plans I have for you," says the Lord. "They are plans for good and not for evil, to give you a future and a hope."
>
> —JEREMIAH 29:11 TLB

We can't go back and we can't stand still. We can move forward in the plans God has for us. We can know that we have the peace and security of God's love and His grace. In that peace we can rest in a future and with hope.

We have to take life as it comes. Each day brings a fresh opportunity to follow the Lord and—in His power and grace—begin life anew from this point forward. Praise His name! The Lord's mercies "are new every morning" (Lamentations 3:23).

So yesterday is yesterday and today is today, and life must be lived with faith and in God's great abundance, joy, and purpose in the 24 hours directly before us.

No matter how much we trust the Lord, no matter how deeply we dip into His resources, there will always, always be more...infinitely more. We can't trust the Lord too much...and all of us trust Him too little.

Even though we look back now and wish we'd realized this more in our younger days, you can actually do something about it in your life now! As a woman, wife, mother, place more of your trust and faith and confidence in God and in His Word. I promise, you'll never regret doing so!

> Experience is not what happens to you, it is what you do with what happens to you.
>
> —ALDOUS HUXLEY

Prayer: Father God, don't let me dwell on what I should have done in the past, but let me be excited about what I can do in the future. Amen.

Action: Look through one of your family photo albums and rejoice over the wonderful family times you had together.

The Power of the Word

The message of the cross is foolishness to those who are perishing,
but to us who are being saved it is the power of God.

1 CORINTHIANS 1:18

All around us are people who believe that Scripture is foolish. They think that people who depend on God and His Word need a crutch to get through life. However, Paul calls the message of the cross "the power of God"—and Scripture presents that message. "Power" is a translation of the Greek word *dunamis,* which our word *dynamite* comes from. Anyone who considers God's Word to be useless will eventually experience the full impact of God. The power of God's Word, when it explodes, leads to a life of freedom.

There's a Chinese tale about a young man who captured a tiger cub, brought it home, and raised it in a cage. When it was full grown, the man bragged about how ferocious and powerful it was. "That tiger isn't wild anymore," scoffed his friends. "He's as tame as an old house cat." This went on until a wise old man overheard them and said, "There's only one way to know whether this tiger is ferocious or not. Open the cage!" The young man smiled, placed his hand on the latch, and challenged his friends, "Want to try out my tiger?"

Even though Scripture may sometimes seem tame and foolish, don't be surprised at its power when it is released into your life.

Prayer: Father God, we have experienced Your power. We thank You for breaking the chain of original sin. Amen.

Action: Understand that God's Word is powerful and destroys the chains of sin.

Makeover of the Heart

Man looks on the outward appearance,
but the Lord looks on the heart.

1 Samuel 16:7 amp

Reality TV is the latest fad in television production. We have all seen them. Many of us have watched and wondered, "How would they change *my* home?" "What would they do with *me?*" I am referring to those extreme makeover programs that are recreating rooms, homes, yards, and even individuals. That's right—individuals.

These shows promise to transform you into your idea of the perfect human being. You could choose a perfect nose, eyes, lips, breasts, thighs, weight—they could change it all so drastically that you wouldn't recognize yourself anymore.

As I leaned back on the sofa, I realized that altering my physical appearance would not change the real me because I reflected on today's Scripture: "Man looks on the outward appearance, but the Lord looks on the heart." "Beauty is only skin deep," but what about the other dimensions of the inner person? The next logical question to ask oneself is, "Am I beautiful in God's sight?" What needs the extreme makeover, my inside or my outside?

In John 3:1-21 Jesus is in deep conversation with a Pharisee named

Nicodemus, a ruler of the Jews, and is explaining the delicate trans-formation of his heart makeover. Jesus explained to Nicodemus that an outward appearance of devotion was simply not enough.

In the conversation that follows Nicodemus finally asks Jesus the all-important question, "How can a man be born again when he is old? Can he enter his mother's womb again and be born?"

Jesus went on to tell this Pharisee that he must be born both of the flesh and the Spirit. Now that is the ultimate extreme makeover.

You might be asking the same question in life. Inside your soul and heart you are yearning for a peace that you aren't experiencing in your everyday life. You look into the mirror, and your physical body looks okay, but there are unsatisfied tensions upon your inner-self.

> There is nothing more certain in Time or Eternity than what Jesus Christ did on the Cross. He switched the whole of the human race back into right relationship with God. He made Redemption the basis of human life, that is, he made a way for every son/daughter of man to get into communion with God. The center of salvation is the Cross of Jesus, and the reason it is so easy to obtain salvation is because it cost God so much.
>
> —OSWALD CHAMBERS

If you find yourself in the same situation as Nicodemus you might go to Romans 10:9-10 and find out how to have an extreme makeover on yourself. It says:

> If you confess with your mouth, "Jesus is Lord," and believe in your heart that God saved Him from the dead, you will be saved. For it is with your heart that you believe and are justified, and it is with your mouth that you confess and are saved.

While we fret over our physical appearance or we waste time ponder-ing what we would change if we had the chance, Jesus is here offering the ultimate makeover, the one that truly does change a person's life, your life—a makeover of the heart.

Prayer: Father God, don't let me get caught up in the world's thought pattern which declares that I should have an extreme makeover. Let me be satisfied with God in how He has created me. However, let me concentrate on my inner qualities that they become more Christlike. Amen.

Action: In your journal list those qualities of Christ's which you want to take on. Work on this makeover.

Hear the Bells

Ascribe to the LORD the glory due to
His name; worship the LORD in holy array.
PSALM 29:2 NASB

A young man from a west Texas farm community received a football scholarship from a small college in Texas. He was very excited about his new adventure. After he had packed his bags to take to school, his mother said good-bye. After her hugs and tears, she asked her son to make her one promise. "Be sure to attend church every Sunday while you are away from home." With no hesitation, he assured his mama he would honor that request.

After settling into his dorm, he met several incoming freshmen he liked. However, these young men had few if any spiritual interests. One of the boys came from a wealthy farm family nearby, and he invited his new friends to come home with him for the weekend to hunt and fish. Of course, the small-town farm boy said, "Yes, that will be fun."

On Sunday morning as they were mounting their horses to go where the hunting and fishing were good, the young man heard the loud bell ring from the nearby church. They rode on farther toward their day's adventure, when again the young man heard a fainter ringing of the church bell. Going farther toward their destination and farther from the church bell, this man again heard the church bell ring, but this time the sound was very faint. He stopped his horse and told his host he had to go back and attend church. The young host said, "We don't have to go to church today. Let's go on, and I'll go to church with you next week." The young man replied, "No, I must go back while I can still hear the bell!"

Are you in that young man's position where you once heard God's strong voice, but today you have moved away from God and His voice is no longer strong but has become fainter and fainter? Your conscience might be calling out, Go back while you can still hear the voice of God!

If you feel far away from God, guess who moved? Return to Him before you no longer hear His voice calling you to come back home.

Prayer: Father God, continue to ring the bell loud and clear. I never want to stop hearing Your call. May everything that would hinder me from hearing Your voice be silenced. Amen.

Action: How clear do you hear the bell ring? If it's not clear, you will want to turn back again to your first love.

Be Thankful and Content in All Things

Bless the LORD, O my soul; and all that is within me,
bless His holy name. Bless the LORD, O my soul,
and forget none of His benefits.

PSALM 103:1-2 NASB

At an early age we begin to teach our children to say "thank you." When someone gives them a gift or compliment—and before they can even utter the words—we jump right in and remind them, "Now what do you say?" However, as we grow from childhood to adulthood, we often forget our manners and hold back from expressing our appreciation to someone who does us a service.

It's the same way with God. He loves to hear and know we are thankful for all He bestows upon us. He is a provider of all we have.

> There is nothing better for a man [woman] than to eat and
> drink and tell himself [herself] that his [her] labor is good.
> This also I have seen that it is from the hand of God. For
> who can eat and who can have enjoyment without Him?
> —ECCLESIASTES 2:24-25

Thankful hearts give thanks. One way to express our thanks for our food is to give a blessing each time we have a meal. Our family always gives a blessing of grace before we eat. This is a tradition at home or out at a restaurant. We never want to forget where our food comes from. We always want to let God know that we appreciate His providing us our food.

As I've gotten older, I look back over this short life and realize that God has been faithful all along the way. He has always provided for all our needs. Not necessarily for our wants but for our needs. That is totally in keeping with the words found in 2 Peter 1:3:

> His divine power has granted to us everything pertaining to life and godliness, through the true knowledge of Him who called us by His own glory and excellence (NASB).

The password for entering into God's presence is "Thank you."

> Enter His gates with thanksgiving and His courts with praise. Give thanks to Him, bless His name.
>
> —PSALM 100:4 NASB

We humbly reach out to God with thanksgiving and praise. One of the leading indicators of our spiritual walk with God is our thankfulness for all He has done for us.

Paul in his writings told us to be content in all situations (Philippians 4:11). When we are restless and find ourselves discontent with our lives and our situations, it's accentuated when we don't have a heart that really gives thanks.

Prayer: Father God, don't let me forget to always be thankful for what You do for me. You are a gracious God who continually pours out blessings on my life. Thank You for everything—big and small. Amen.

Action: Evaluate the thankfulness of your heart. How could it be improved?

The Strength to Change

If anyone is in Christ he is a new creation;
the old has gone, the new has come!

2 Corinthians 5:17

They say that you can't teach an old dog to change, but I want to tell you that that's not true. In fact if you do something for 21 consecutive days, you can create a new habit. We as individuals must realize that we no longer want to be as we have been. In the same way, since knowing Jesus I realize that I no longer like my old self.

Becoming a woman of God begins with making a personal commitment to Jesus Christ. Only He can give us the fresh start that allows the spirit to grow strong in us.

Second Corinthians 5:17 reminds us, "If anyone is in Christ, he is a new creation; the old has gone, the new has come!" That's what I discovered many years ago when I, a 16-year-old Jewish girl, received Christ into my heart. My life began to change from that moment on and the years since then have always been an exciting adventure.

> The desire of the sluggard puts him to death, for his hands
> refuse to work; all day long he is craving, while the righteous
> gives and does not hold back.
>
> —Proverbs 21:25-26 nasb

It hasn't always been easy. I've had to give up much bitterness, anger, fear, hatred, and resentment. Many times I've had to back up and start over asking God to take over control of my life and show me His way to live. But as I have learned to follow Him, He has guided me through times of pain and joy, struggle and growth. And how rewarding it has been to see growth take root and grow in my life. I give thanks and praise for all His goodness to me over the years.

I'm not finished yet—far from it. Growing in godliness is a lifelong process. Although God is the One who makes it possible, He requires my cooperation. If I want to be more Godlike and to have this shine in my life and in my home, I must be willing to change what God wants me to change and learn what He wants to teach me.

Prayer: Father God, I realize that change is possible. Give me the strength to become more like You! Amen.

Action: In your journal list three things you want to change about yourself. Then beside each one state what you are going to do to make that change possible.

When You Want to Ask "Why"

God is our refuge and strength, always ready to
help in times of trouble. So we will not fear when
earthquakes come and the mountains crumble into the sea.

PSALM 46:1-2 NLT

When disaster strikes in a far away land, when someone we know faces serious illness, when we are left heartbroken after a great loss, it can shake our faith to its core. Have you ever shouted out to God, asking where He was in the time of need? Have you cried with deep grief and questioned how God could let something so bad happen?

It seems to be very human to ask this "Why?" question at such times. Our inquiring minds want to know. Why would a loving God permit destruction, devastation, and death?

The sad fact is, we live in a fallen world, and events happen according to the laws of nature. Because of the sin of mankind there will always be things that happen other than what we would want—a perfect world. There will be troubles and suffering beyond our control. At such times, our comfort must come from God's Word.

In today's verse we find three comforts in such events of life:

- God is our refuge.

- God is our strength.
- God is always ready to help in times of trouble.

If we can internalize these "big three" promises we can live with this victory:

- We will not live in fear.

What great assurance when our soul quakes. We can apply these promises to all events of life—tsunamis, earthquakes, heartbreaks, or soul quakes.

Just remember, when we walk through life's storms we have two alternatives:

- Respond as a faith-filled person.
- Respond as a faithless person.

> How blessed is the man who does not walk in the counsel of the wicked, nor stand in the path of sinners, nor sit in the seat of scoffers! But his delight is in the law of the LORD, and in the law he meditates day and night, and he will be like a tree firmly planted by streams of water, which yields its fruit in its season and its leaf does not wither; and whatever he does, he prospers.
>
> —PSALM 1:1-3 NASB

A faith-filled person will respond in these ways:

- She delights in reading and knowing God's Word.
- She meditates on God's law day and night.
- She will be like a tree firmly planted by streams of water.
- She yields fruit in its season.
- Her leaves will not wither.
- She will prosper in all things.

This woman of faith understands where she comes from and where she is going. She is not one who questions God because of the events of the world. She doesn't look to the world for the answers of life. She is firmly grounded in what God assures her, even when the quakes of life occur.

Prayer: Father God, let me stand on Your promises when the hardships of life come my way, as they surely will. Give me the faith to trust Your Word. Amen.

Action: Begin today to trust God and all of His promises for you and your family. Reread Psalm 1:2-3.

Be a Woman of Serenity

In recent years we have been told and obsessed with
figuring out what a woman should be allowed to
do. God says in His Word a woman can do anything;
the point is not what she does but what she is.

ANNE ORTLUND

The dictionary defines serene as "calm, clear, unruffled, peaceful, placid, tranquil, and unperturbed." Do these words describe any place or any one you may know? Maybe the Grand Canyon? And maybe a wise woman who has discovered the peace of our Lord and learned how to rest in Him? That dictionary definition of serene describes so few places and people in today's world. We have fast-food restaurants, drive-through lines, car phones, second-day mail, next day mail, facsimile machines, BlackBerries®, and iPhones—at home and even in the car.

We yearn for peace and quiet, but where do we turn? We must turn to God. We have to become quiet inside. Chuck Swindoll comments about the quietness we need today:

> You know something? That still, small voice will never shout. God's methods don't change because we are so noisy

and busy. He is longing for your attention, your undivided and full attention. He wants to talk with you in times of quietness (with the TV off) about your need for understanding love, compassion, patience, self-control, a calm spirit, genuine humility...and wisdom. But He won't run to catch up. He will wait and wait until you finally sit in silence and listen.[4]

We need to be quiet before the Lord, to experience His peace and His restoring touch. We need to listen to what He would teach us and hear where He would have us go. We will benefit greatly from such times with our heavenly Father. Your peaceful calm will be restored.

> Order and the beauty of peace go together. The fair flower of peace does not grow among the weeds of an ill-regulated life. The radiance of a deep inner serenity is the product of disciplining both in the heart and in outward affairs.
> —G.H. Morling

A man responds well to a woman who is serene. She settles the environment just by her presence; she is at peace with those around her. A serene woman is sensitive to nature, aware of all aspects of her womanhood, and willing to help make the world better. She is not so rushed that she can't give her husband and family her time. Her home will reflect this serenity, encouraging people to relax. Guests will ask, "How do you ever leave this home? It is so comfortable! I feel such tranquility when I'm with you, and it's so good to relax." Has anyone told you this lately?

Here are some expressions of love:

- Buy some new lingerie for tonight—or that weekend getaway!
- Bake a batch of chocolate chip cookies for your family.
- Greet your husband at the door with a kiss.

- Make your home a special place to be: buy fresh or silk flowers; use soft, gentle-smelling potpourri, and so on.

- Create a pleasing, romantic aroma for your mate by lingering in a bathtub spiced with fragrant oils.

"A woman without serenity seems hardly like a woman at all," says Dr. Toni Grant. "She is nervous, high-strung, all bent out of shape and utterly impatient."

One key to finding serenity is learning to let life happen around you. You don't have to be involved in everything. Sometimes it is very right to say, "No." Let go of those things you can't control. Serenity and tranquility are gifts from God. They come when we trust Him as our Lord, Shepherd, Guide, and Protector.

Prayer: Father God, I want to be able to slow down and become serene in my life. Place me around ladies who will hold me accountable to this desire. Amen.

Action:

- Turn on some peaceful music.
- Take a walk around the neighborhood.
- Take a warm bubble bath.
- Speak quietly and smile when you talk.
- Sit in a quiet room for five minutes. Reflect on what God is doing in your life.

Be a Light Wherever You Are

You are the light of the world.
A city on a hill cannot be hidden.
MATTHEW 5:14

The parlor was tiny, just an extra room behind the store. But the tablecloth was spotless, the candles were glowing, the flowers were bright, the tea was fragrant. Most of all the smile was genuine and welcoming whenever my mother invited people to "come on back for a cup of tea."

How often I heard her say those words when I was growing up. And how little I realized the mark they would make on me.

Those were hard years after my father died, when Mama and I shared three rooms behind our little dress shop in Long Beach, California. Mama waited on the customers, did alternations, and worked on the books until late at night. I kept house—planning and shopping for meals, cooking, cleaning, doing laundry—while going to school and learning the dress business as well.

Sometimes I felt like Cinderella—work, work, work. And the little girl in me longed for a Prince Charming to carry me away to his castle. There I would preside over a grand and immaculate household, waited on hand and foot by attentive servants. I would wear gorgeous dresses and entertain kings and queens who marveled at my beauty and my wisdom and brought me lavish gifts.

But in the meantime, of course, I had work to do. And although I didn't know it, I was already receiving a gift more precious than any dream castle could be. For unlike Cinderella, I lived with a loving mama who understood the true meaning of sharing and of joy—a mama who brightened people's lives with an unusual ability to make people feel comfortable when they were around her.

> Let your light shine before men, that they may see your
> good deeds and praise your Father in heaven.
>
> MATTHEW 5:16

Our customers quickly learned that Mama offered a sympathetic ear as well as elegant clothes and impeccable service. Often they ended up sharing their hurts and problems with her. And then, inevitably, would come the invitation, "Let me make you a cup of tea." She would usher our guests back to our living room/kitchen. Quickly a fresh cloth was slipped on the table, a candle lit, fresh flowers set out, and the teapot heated. If we had them, she would pull out cookies or a loaf of banana bread. There was never anything fancy, but the gift of her caring warmed many a heart on a cold afternoon.

And Mama didn't limit her hospitality to just guests. On many a rainy day I came home from school to a hot baked potato, fresh from the oven. Even with her heavy workload, Mama would take the time to make this little Cinderella feel like a queen.

My mama's willingness to open her life to others—to share her home, her food, and her love—was truly a royal gift. She passed it along to me, and I have the privilege of passing it on to others. What a joy to carry on her gift of entertaining strangers and friends.

Prayer: Father God, thank You for giving me a mama who cared for others. She modeled to me the true spirit of hospitality. Thanks for her being a part of my life. Amen.

Action: Share a hot cup of tea with someone today.

House Hunting

In My Father's house are many mansions...
I go to prepare a place for you.
JOHN 14:2 NKJV

There are different passages a couple travels through life. I clearly recall when we realized that we had to sell the "Barnes' Barn" after 16 years and move back to Newport Beach, California, where my oncologist practiced medicine. It was a very tearful experience to leave our home after all these years, but we knew we couldn't keep up our property while we were concentrating on the healing journey.

Looking for that new perfect home is another adventure. Each of us were drawn to different houses. Our realtors, bless their patience, kept showing us homes on the market. Then one day our sales rep called and said she had the perfect house to show us. It met all the qualifications on our wish list. Sure enough, it was just what we were looking for!

How thankful we are that, as Christians, we do not have this problem regarding our heavenly home. Jesus assures us that He has already located, purchased, and closed escrow on our mansion in heaven. He promises to take us there to be with His Father forever. What a comfort to know that when believing loved ones die they have moved into that perfect home made just for them. No "For Sale" signs on the lawn; they are ushered into their heavenly home to spend eternity with their Lord.

Prayer: Father God, thank You for assuring us that You have gone before us and paid the price for our eternal salvation. We look forward to being with You in heaven. Amen.

Action: Praise God for His heavenly provision for you and your family. Rest in the knowledge that you have a mansion on high.

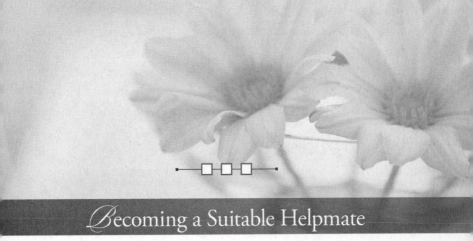

Becoming a Suitable Helpmate

*Then the LORD God said, "It is not good for the man to
be alone. I will make him a helper suitable for him."*
GENESIS 2:18

"Bob, would you mind helping me move this table? I'm not strong enough!" He loves to know that I need him. Men love to be needed—they respond in a very positive fashion during those times of emergencies.

In our Western culture, we women consider ourselves to be very capable. We pride ourselves on our self-sufficiency and ability to get things done. We don't need help from anyone! That is as true for women as it is for men.

Many women today are hard charging, assertive, and very competent. Yet the wise woman of the twenty-first century is beginning to slow down. She has realized that enough's enough, and she is giving up her attempt to be superwoman and/or supermom. She has realized that the elusive goal of doing and being all things isn't worth what it's costing her to try to reach it. Free of society's unrealistic expectations and its call to be independent, such a woman can say, "Honey, I need you. Would you please help me?"

One way to melt a man's heart is to show him that you truly need him. The simple, direct statement, "I need your help," reinforces your husband's masculinity.

Scripture teaches the importance of having someone there to help us when we are in need. The writer of Ecclesiastes notes that "two are better than one because they have a good return for their labor. If one falls down, his [her] friend can help him [her] up. But pity the man [woman] who falls and has no one to help him [her] up" (4:9-10). In Galatians 6:2, Paul calls believers to "bear one another's burdens, and thus fulfill the law of Christ" (NASB). Again and again Scripture reminds us of the importance of having someone come alongside to help when times are difficult. Reaching out helps our needs to be met and also creates a special bond with the person we let come near.

In creation God created woman to be a helpmate for her husband. Genesis 2:18 reads, "It is not good for the man to be alone; I will make him a helper suitable for him."

My question to married women is: "Are you a helper or hindrance to your husband?" God created us to help our husbands in all that they do. My observation as I read, study, and observe is that American women have lost the focus of making their husbands their heroes.

Take time to be an encourager to your spouse; let them know that you appreciate all they do for you and their family. Let them know that you are glad to see them come home to be with the family.

Prayer: Father God, I truly want to be a helpmate for my husband. I want to fulfill the commission that God has given to me from creation. Guide me in the proper direction. Amen.

Action: Write a note of encouragement to your husband. Put it in his lunch, suitcase as he travels, or upon his pillow. Lift him up.

A Time for Everything

He hath made everything
beautiful in his time.
ECCLESIASTES 3:11 KJV

Ralph Waldo Emerson said it so well: "Finish every day and be done with it. You have done what you could. Some blunders and absurdities no doubt crept in; forget them as soon as you can. Tomorrow is a new day; begin it well and serenely and with too high a spirit to be cumbered with old nonsense. This day is all that is good and fair. It is too dear, with its hopes and invitations, to waste a moment on yesterday."

Truly there is a season for everything. Behind every happening, there is a purpose. Nothing happens by accident. Life flows through its natural cycles. There is a time to be born, a beginning, and a time to die, an ending. God has a divine timetable.

When my mother-in-law passed away we were richly blessed by knowing that her cycle of life on earth had been completed as God has planned. We knew that through the years, God had turned every ugly event in her life beautiful. And now she was trading her earthly life for one in which there is no more pain.

During her life she had heartaches and laughter, along with sickness and health. There were no "whys" when she passed away. We knew that it was all part of God's cycle for her. When we realize that God has a timing for everything, then we can trust that everything will be beautiful in His perfect time.

Prayer: Lord of Time and Life, You are the Alpha and the Omega. You are the beginning and the end. Help me be patient and learn to live at peace with Your timetable. Let me not rush my agenda. Let me trust You more. Amen.

Action: Slow down this week so that you can better observe what God is unfolding in your life. Don't rush everything, even when it is tempting. Trust God's timing and consider the times that you are waiting as opportunities to rest in God's peace and His purpose.

Be on the Winning Team

Do you not know that
those who run in a race all run,
but one receives the prize?
Run in such a way that you may win.
1 Corinthians 9:24 NASB

The world has gone crazy with sports. Twenty-four hours a day you can view some athletic event: baseball, football, basketball, swimming, soccer, volleyball, and track, to name a few. I can remember when ESPN announced that they were going to create a 24/7 sports channel. My Bob said very prophetically, "There's not enough sports to fill their programming." Boy, was his prophecy off. Any day—any time of the day—there are sporting events shown from around the world.

Sporting events on TV are so easily found while surfing the channels that we have become knowledgeable about a multitude of different activities. From our armchair, we sometimes think we could accomplish what we watch others do. But the 63 for Tiger Woods, the 42 points for Kobe Bryant, or the three home runs by Hank Aaron are phenomenal feats that few can duplicate.

Paul is a favorite biblical character because he was an outstanding competitor and someone who would never quit. What made his career so amazing was that while he was an ardent, follow-the-law Pharisee, he had made it his job to rid the world of Christians. But on his way to Damascus to bring back some of the captured Christians for trial, Paul had a marvelous encounter with God. Paul is the person who penned so many books of the New Testament. He encourages us to run the race to win. In order for us to win the contest, we must deny ourselves many things that would keep us from doing our best. An athlete goes to all the trouble to win the prize, but we do it for a heavenly reward that never disappears.

Paul knew what it took to be a champion. He says that in a race, everyone runs but only one person wins first prize—so run your race to win. We are all striving to be the people God created us to be and to share God's message of love. Paul's teaching shares:

- If you're going to take the challenge—win.
- We will pay a price to be a winner.

In today's language we would express:

- No pain, no gain!
- There is no easy way to success. It's hard work!

Recipe for success:

- Study while others are sleeping;
- Work while others are loafing;
- Prepare while others are playing;
- Dream while others are wishing.

—William A. Ward

Prayer: Father God, give me the excitement needed to run the race to win. I don't want to be just a spectator of life. I want to be a real participant who is willing to pay the price for being a servant to those in need. Amen.

Action: Go out and discipline your life for that heavenly reward.

Be an Attractive Spouse

Don't be concerned about the outward beauty
that depends on jewelry, or beautiful clothes,
or hair arrangement. Be beautiful inside, in your
hearts, with the lasting charm of a gentle and
quiet spirit that is so precious to God.

1 PETER 3:3-5 TLB

Scripture calls a woman to be godly and to develop an inward beauty, but wise women also work to make themselves pleasing to their husbands' eyes—and that's right on target. Now, as a woman, you might not feel that the externals are very important, but doesn't looking nice make you feel better about yourself? Furthermore, externals are important because men are sexually aroused by visual stimulation. When men aren't proud of what they see in their wives, they become more vulnerable to having an affair. A pleasing appearance will invite your husband to touch and to hold you—and no one else.

Besides, your husband wants to be proud that you're by his side whether at home or in public. Every married woman needs to ask herself, "Am I looking my best when I am with my husband? Is he proud of my personal appearance?" If you feel you could make yourself more appealing and attractive, know that the resources available are many, ranging from self-help books, friends who will give suggestions, color and wardrobe seminars, and department store consultants who will assist you in developing a new you.

I encourage you to pay attention to how you look for your husband. You, your husband, and your marriage will definitely benefit!

Prayer: Father God, help me to have a balanced life between my inner and outward beauty. Let me reach out and learn some things that will be beneficial in both areas of my life. Amen.

Action: Go to the cosmetic counter in your local department store and have them give you some basic help in improving your outward appearance.

Respect

*Nevertheless, each individual among you also is
to love his own wife even as himself, and his wife
must see to it that she respects her husband.*

EPHESIANS 5:33 NASB

Shortly after we began working together, Bob and I were doing a seminar at a church. He was going back and forth from the car, carrying in the book table and boxes of books and other materials. Out in the parking lot, a woman who thought she was being clever said to him, "Oh, you must be Mr. Emilie Barnes."

What did this remark do to his ego? He laughed it off at the time, but inside he struggled. And through the years he's occasionally had to wrestle with the fact that I'm usually the one who is more well-known and upfront in our public ministry. He remains behind the scenes doing the logistics and legwork.

Bob has dealt with it because he knows that, for now, those are the roles God has given us, and this is where we are in life. I'm so proud of him for the way he's balanced his masculine ego needs with his servant's heart and love for Jesus Christ. His attitude encourages me to redouble my efforts to let him know that I need him, that he means everything to me, and that I couldn't go on in ministry without him.

Your man wants to know you truly admire and respect him. He may not get much respect at work, he may not get respect from the guys on his softball team, he may not get respect from his dad or mom or brothers and sisters, but you can shower him with respect and admiration.

In fact, that is exactly what the Bible tells us. Speaking to husbands and wives, the apostle Paul says, "Nevertheless, each individual among you also is to love his own wife even as himself, and the wife must see to it that she respects her husband" (Ephesians 5:33 NASB). Isn't it interesting that in this verse men are commanded to love their wives with an unselfish love, but Paul doesn't turn right around and say (as you might anticipate), "And wives, make sure you love your husbands too"? No, the apostle makes the point that the wife needs to first of all show her husband respect. The Greek word Paul uses here for respect actually means "to revere" or "to be in awe of."

Obviously this could be carried to a ridiculous extreme, but I think what Paul is saying is that the wife must see to it that she honors her husband in her mind and in her actions. She needs to make sure she's not disrespecting, ridiculing, undercutting, or ignoring him. Respecting your husband is one of those biblical commands that goes directly cross-grain to political correctness and popular culture. You don't have to watch very many movies, TV shows, or commercials to see that men—particularly married men and fathers—are portrayed as bumbling, fumbling, selfish, and stupid. It's always hip and smart these days to mock men and masculinity. And the idea of a wife truly respecting—actually revering—her husband? Well, what a preposterous, stone-age idea that would be.

But true followers of Jesus Christ have always been at odds with prevailing attitudes. Our Lord calls us to be radiant lights in a dark, dreary place and salt in a bland, tasteless world. Being wives who respect their husbands in the name and power of Christ is a mighty witness for Him in these perilous times.

How can you let your husband know he's your Superman? Occasionally ask him to help you in ways that make him feel strong. Maybe you could remove that jar lid if you banged on it, ran it under hot water, and worked on it for a while. But hand it to your husband. There isn't a husband in the world who doesn't feel good about using his strength to open a jar for his wife. Ask him to help you bring in the groceries. You could do this job very well yourself, but once in a while say, "Honey, will you please help me bring these groceries in?" That's one way of telling him that he's the strong one, and he's the guy you depend on.

Make your man Superman, and he will make you Super-woman![5]

> Choose a good reputation over great riches; being held in
> high esteem is better than silver or gold.
> —Proverbs 22:1 nlt

Prayer: Father God, may I remember to respect my husband, be an encourager, and a supporter of his dreams. Amen.

Action: Tell your husband how much you appreciate all he does for your family.

$\mathcal{T}$hirty-five Years of Prayer

Rejoice always, pray without ceasing, in everything give
thanks; for this is the will of God in Christ Jesus for you.

1 THESSALONIANS 5:16-18 NKJV

$\mathcal{B}$ob and I have a dear friend who has stood by her husband when his heart was hard against God. I met Ruth at church, but we were both involved in the Christian Women's Association. Ruth was a very proper and elegant lady and the model of hospitality. When a person went to her home for dinner or a Sunday brunch, you thought you were at the Ritz-Carlton Hotel. Her speech and body language had the polish of a fine finishing school.

Her husband, George, on the other hand, was a self-made oil executive. He had started out working on the oil rigs in Bakersfield, California, and earned his wealth through hard work and good investments. His manners were rough and his speech was punctuated with four-letter words and God's good name occasionally thrown in.

> There are many who want me to tell them of secret ways
> of becoming perfect and I can only tell them that the sole
> secret is a hearty love of God, and the only way of attaining
> that love is by loving. You learn to speak by speaking, to

study by studying, to run by running, to work by working; and just so you learn to love God and man by loving. Begin as a mere apprentice and the very power of love will lead you on to become a master of the art.

—St. Francis of Sales

Ruth and George seemed to be at opposite ends of the spectrum not just in manners but in their relationship to the Lord as well. Ruth shared that she had prayed every day for George's salvation for 34 years, and he didn't seem any closer to knowing the Lord than he had on the day they were married. Bob and I also began to pray for George, and when it became clear that George enjoyed our company, we invited Ruth and George to our home Bible study. When George said yes, we were all startled beyond belief. And you better believe that we were rejoicing!

Ruth and George came faithfully every Wednesday night for a year. During that time, George also started coming to church, signed up for the men's retreat, and one Sunday morning accepted Jesus as his personal Savior. Ruth had faithfully prayed for 35 years for George to know the Lord—and God answered her prayers.

How do we respond when Jesus tarries two years plus when we pray fervently for our loved ones? Do we be still and know that God's timetable is different than our calendar?

Prayer: Father God, give me patience so I can continue to pray for those who need to know Jesus. I know You hear me and will act upon my petitions. Thank You for the miracle You are performing in my life. Amen.

Action:

Your husband the positive and God the negative.

—Ruth Graham

ℒet Go of That Anxiety

I say to you, do not be worried about your life, as to
what you will eat or what you will drink; nor for your
body, as to what you shall put on. Is not life more
than food, and the body more than clothing?

MATTHEW 6:25

𝓘 don't know about where you live, but in Southern California we tend to lead anxious lives. Although we have it much easier than our parents did, we certainly are much more uneasy about our life than they were.

For instance, my parents never cared much about going out to eat at the latest in-vogue restaurant, or vacationing at the new island hotel with the larger pool than the previous one. They didn't work out to keep their shape nor make sure they wore the latest hot logo on their shirts and sweaters. And they wanted a car that would run efficiently, but it didn't have to be the hottest brand on the market. (It could even be American-made.) And it didn't have to be an SUV or have four-wheel drive and a plush interior.

Yes, today there seems to be a lot of pressure to make sure we keep up with the latest trends in search of the perfect life.

Take a hard look at the message from the modern media and you'll see what I mean. Most of the advertisements try to persuade us that what we wear and what restaurants we eat at and the cars we drive will determine who we are.

Our modern culture has built itself around a mind-set that causes us to be more concerned over life's accommodations along life's journey than with our final destination.

Because of all these false messages, we may look good on the outside, but we have a vast emptiness on the inside. We have all the trimmings of a great life. We have the best-dressed families, the finest homes, great-paying jobs. We go to all the five-star resorts, our garages are filled with the finest cars, we have all the latest and finest sporting gear, but we find ourselves anxious. Inside, we aren't satisfied with who we have become.

> Blessed are those who trust in the LORD...They are like
> trees planted along a riverbank, with roots that reach deep
> into the water. Such trees are not bothered by the heat or
> worried by long months of drought. Their leaves stay green,
> and they never stop producing fruit.
>
> —JEREMIAH 17:7-8 NLT

We come to a stage in life where we realize this thing called life is more important than food, and the body is more important than what we wear. We come to realize that all these things don't satisfy the soul and have become cheap substitutes for spiritual wholeness and well-being.

When one loses sight of who God is and forgets to give Him honor, anxiety sets in and day-to-day living doesn't make sense. When we make things our goal in life and take our eyes off Jesus, we invariably will be disappointed. Anxious people need to turn their eyes on Christ and worship Him. I have found that He has never failed me in my journey. He gives me moderation and balance to my life.

One of our family's favorite verses is Matthew 6:33: "Seek first His kingdom and His righteousness, and all these things shall be added to you" (NASB). Yes, this is the "anxiety breaker"—seek first His kingdom. Bob and I try to make this verse our test for doing anything in life. With this decision that needs to be made, are we truly seeking His kingdom first—or are we doing it just for ourselves?

> Anxiety is the natural result when our hopes are centered on anything short of God and his will for us.
>
> —BILLY GRAHAM

In John 16:33 we read, "These things I have spoken to you, so that in Me you may have peace. In the world you have tribulation, but take courage; I have overcome the world" (NASB). God has promised us peace, but many of us choose anxiety instead. Possessions will never give us satisfaction in life.

We will never be the people God wants us to be until we heed His call: "Come to Me...and I will give you rest."

Let Christ help you overcome the anxieties of life. He will help you to...

- Stop chasing the temporal things of life. Seek the kingdom of God as it is revealed in Jesus. Cast all your cares on Him.
- Take your eyes off yourself and focus them on God first. Many of our anxieties are rooted in our self-centeredness.
- Spend most of your prayer time in praying for others. Keep yourself away from most of your prayers.
- Do not continue to straddle the fence. Commit your total efforts and energy to Christ.[6]

Prayer: Father God, take my eyes off the things of the world. I realize life is more than possessions. I have had them and they don't give purpose and meaning to my life. I want to focus on serving You all of

my days. Give me the strength and conviction to
follow Your ways. Amen.

Action: Analyze what is making you anxious. What are
you going to do about it? Write out in your journal
what these anxieties are and what you will do to
change each into peace.

The Rewards of Friendship

He who has found his life will lose it, and he
who has lost his life for My sake will find it.

MATTHEWS 10:39 NASB

*Y*ou probably don't need to be convinced, but friendship does indeed offer rich rewards. Consider the comments of these people:

- Upon the death of his friend A. H. Hallam, the poet Tennyson declared, "'Tis better to have loved and lost than never to have loved at all."

- Helen Keller once said, "With the death of every friend I have loved a part of me has been buried but their contribution to my being of happiness, strength and understanding remains to sustain me in an altered world."

- Jesus taught that we find ourselves when we lose ourselves (Matthew 10:39).

When have you experienced these truths about friendship? The value of friendship extends beyond emotional closeness and connectedness. Research, for instance, shows that lonely people live significantly shorter lives than their counterparts.

What do you think of when you think of friendship? Intimate sharing? Talking about feelings and hurts and hopes?

The fact seems to stand that women have an easier time with friendships than men do. Our culture, for instance, permits women to be closer to each other than men can be with one another. Women can hug, cry, hold hands, and interlock their arms as they walk down the street, but men are not as free to do these things.

> It is the steady and merciless increase of occupations, the augmented speed at which we are always trying to live, the crowding of each day with more work than it can profitably hold, which has cost us, among other things, the undisturbed enjoyment of friends. Friendship takes time, and we have no time to give it.
>
> —AGNES REPPLIER

Friendships are another difference between men and women. Men are activity-oriented and women are relationally-oriented. How can you bridge that gap? Simply get interested in your husband's activities. That's one way you can be his friend. After all, "You have to be a friend in order to have a friend."

Prayer: Father God, I realize that there is a difference between how men and women look at friendship. May I have the proper discernment to make my husband my friend. Amen.

Action: Take your husband on a date and watch one of his favorite kind of movies. Get an ice-cream cone after the movie.

Knowing the Father's Heart

*For it is God who works in you to will and
to act according to his good purpose.*

PHILIPPIANS 2:13

One of the great mysteries of prayer is why some are healed and not others. Why do some get miracles and others are left terminally ill? After endless months and years of petitioning to God, we have come to the realization that "God's will" will be done. He has a wonderful timetable for each of our lives. The sooner we recognize this in our Christian walk the quicker we will understand that His thoughts are greater than our thoughts and His ways are greater than our ways.

As I've said earlier, God healed me of my mantle cell lymphoma, and we give praises to Him for that. We claimed John 11:4 as our theme verse: "This sickness will not end in death. No, it is for God's glory so that God's Son may be glorified through it."

This declaration came about over years and years of previous prayers and the study of God's Word that proved we could trust God for everything—yes, even our lives. Through historical observation we knew God had our personal interest in His command. This kind of faith makes life so exciting. We don't have to search the world over for the purpose of life, we have found it and are living it daily. The

Westminster Confession of Faith expresses it very clearly: "Man's chief end is to glorify God, and to enjoy Him forever." Prayer helps establish this purpose of life for us. Without this we would still have a holy God but no reason for why we are here on earth.

If we are to live meaningful lives we have the two options that Jesus gave His disciples in Luke 18:1: We are to pray and not lose heart. Around us are a Father's arms, and we are to cry out to Him because, in Jesus, His voice has already called out to us. We are to answer like children crying out to their father. Because, like children, we do not always know what is wrong with us.

When we face the many pressures of life, there is only one way out—we are to pray. Prayer is our way to the place of power; it is the way to certain solutions of our problems. Yes—it's an answer to all of our unbearable pressures. Prayer is crying out to our God we cannot see but whom we rely upon, a Father with a father's heart and a father's tender compassion and willingness to act. Prayer always stirs the heart of God. Prayer always moves God to act.

The answer to a prayer request may indeed be long delayed, but there is no delay at all in an answer to the prayer itself. When we cry out there is immediately an answer—speedily God rushes to help. The answer may be the squeeze of the Father's hand on ours, the quiet comfort of the Father's voice, the reassurance of the Father's presence even though the stresses and pressures are still evident.

The purpose of prayer is to bring us into an understanding of the Father's heart. It brings us not always to the place of an answer, but to the place where a direct answer is unnecessary to an understanding of God's will for our lives. We cannot establish a relationship with God without communication. Human desires and needs require "speech." Prayer is an absolute necessity in the interchange of a believer's heart with the Father. Martin Luther once cried out, "O Father, teach us to pray."

Prayer: Father God, our communion table has etched into its wood, "This Do in Remembrance of Me." May I never forget Your faithfulness in the past, and Your faithfulness in the present, so I can trust Your faithfulness for the future. Amen.

Action: Remind yourself of times you have witnessed God's faithfulness. Share about these times with someone who needs to hear of His goodness.

You Are Known by Your Choices

If any of you lacks wisdom, let him ask God, who gives to all men
generously and without reproach, and it will be given to him.

JAMES 1:5

I tell the women who attend my seminars that there are three things that determine what each of us will be in five years:

- the people we meet
- the books we read
- the choices we make

I like to emphasize the third one because so often we forget how our choices have such a significant impact on us, our lives, and the lives of our loved ones. The choices we make determine who we are now and who we will be in the future. The more wisdom one has, the better choices they will make. I have found that any wisdom I may have is that which I have gained from reading and studying the holy Scriptures. Anything else I consider knowledge. Knowledge is much easier and faster to acquire than wisdom. Gaining wisdom is a lifelong pursuit and cannot be attained in a college class or through a search on the Internet.

The Bible is full of wonderful assurances and promises for all who believe in Jesus Christ, the Son of God. But each person must choose Jesus as his/her own Savior before they can claim these promises personally. How can these promises be yours?

The Bible says that we are to...

Recognize that you cannot be saved by trying to be good or because you are doing the best you can, or because you are a member of a social or religious organization. God says we are not saved by our good works:

> By grace you have been saved, through faith—and this not of yourselves, it is the gift of God—not by works, so that no one should boast.
>
> —Ephesians 2:8-9

Confess that you cannot save yourself, that you are a guilty sinner worthy of God's righteous judgment, and that you are hopelessly lost without the Lord Jesus Christ as your personal Savior.

Believe the good news that Jesus died for the ungodly (Romans 5:8). He also died for you and settled your sins debt by His death on Calvary's cross. Believe the blessed news that Christ was raised from the dead and now lives to save all who will come to Him in faith.

Call on the name of the Lord Jesus Christ with a sincere desire to be saved from your sins. God has promised that "whosoever shall call upon the name of the Lord shall be saved" (Romans 10:13 KJV).

Rely upon God's sure promise, not upon your feelings. By faith declare you are saved by the blood of Jesus Christ, shed for the forgiveness of your sins. Openly confess Him as your Lord and Savior.

> God so loved the world, that He gave His only begotten Son, that whoever believes in Him shall not perish but have eternal life.
>
> —John 3:16

If you have never put your faith in Jesus as your personal Savior, I encourage you to do it right now in the quietness of your own heart.

Prayer: Father God, I realize I'm a sinner and separated from You. I open my heart to receive You as my personal Savior and Lord of my life. I know You will forgive me of my sins. I want You to be my mentor and to give me guidance and purpose for life. I want You to be the Potter, and I will be the clay. Mold me and make me in Your own way. Amen.

Action: Start making good choices today. You will be known by the decisions you make and the paths you choose.

Clear Out the Prayer Closet

Very early in the morning, while it was still dark, Jesus got up,
left the house and went off to a solitary place, where he prayed.

MARK 1:35

Charles Spurgeon once said, "Do not learn the language of prayer, but seek the spirit of prayer, and God almighty will bless you and make you more mighty in your supplications." Every so often, we need to evaluate what's happening in our prayer lives. This way we can catch ourselves if we're slipping in our purpose and direction. Sometimes our prayers and methods become routine—not much is happening that's really meaningful. Maybe the hinges to your "prayer closet" door are rusty, but they do open and shut at their appointed times. Perhaps the doors are locked and cobwebbed. Or maybe you do not neglect prayer itself, but what a tale the walls might tell! "Oh!" the walls cry out. "We have heard you when you have been in such a rush that you could hardly spend two minutes with God. We have witnessed you coming and spending ten minutes and not asking for anything—at least your heart did not ask. The lips moved, but the heart was silent. We have heard you groan out of your soul, but we have seen you go away distrustful, not believing your prayer was heard, quoting the promise, but not thinking God would fulfill it."

We find ourselves going through the motions of prayer but not really praying. It's sort of like driving down the freeway at 65 miles per hour and not remembering the landscape that has whizzed by. We need to slow down and clear out the cobwebs from our minds as we kneel before God. He deserves our utmost awareness as we come before Him. Get excited about prayer time! Pay attention, be alert, stay awake.

Prayer: Father God, may I go beyond the language of formal prayer, to seek the Spirit of prayer. May You bless me and honor my supplications. Amen.

Action: Create a warm-up ritual before you pray. Prepare a prayer closet or choose a favorite chair, dim the lights, and curl up with a blanket as you speak to your heavenly Father.

Pruning Hurts

Every branch that bears fruit he prunes
so that it will be even more fruitful.

JOHN 15:2

My Bob is a real believer in pruning all our trees and shrubs each year. I can't stand to go outside on those days. For years I have said something like, "Bob, you are killing the plants. They will never grow back." And for the same number of years Bob has replied, "Emilie, you wait and see. In a few weeks the plants will be more beautiful than before." And you know what? Every year the plants have come back more beautiful than before!

Throughout Palestine, vines grow abundantly, and every year gardeners prune the branches in order to produce high quality fruit. Branches are considered useless unless they produce. Fruitless vines are drastically cut back, and the pruned limbs are destroyed. The Old Testament pictures Israel as the vineyard of God, so the vine became a symbol for the people of God. Jesus called Himself the true vine, using the vine and branches as an analogy to show how a believer must abide in Him. Jesus' followers who believed in Him were the branches on God's vine. The branches had no source of life within themselves, but they received life from the vine. Without the vine, the branches could produce no fruit.

Perhaps, at times, you feel like a shrub being pruned. You want to cry out, "Stop! I've had enough!" When you cry out, you may hear God say, "I'm answering your prayers. The unnecessary—the unproductive—must be cut off from your life so that the fruit will appear. Pruning is necessary in nature, and it is necessary in your life as My child." Remember it is your God who is doing the pruning. Pruning is a painful process, but it does not last forever. One day your cut branches will sprout forth new growth and fruit will appear.

Prayer: Father God, let us listen to You when You are pruning our lives. Let us not yell stop, but look at the shears and know that You have our best in mind. We look forward to bearing new fruit. Amen.

Action: Trust your Master Gardener when He is pruning your branches.

Loving One Another

Two are better than one, because they have a good return
for their work. If one falls down, his friend can help him up.
But pity the man who falls and has no one to help him up.

ECCLESIASTES 4:9-10

You would think that after so many years of marriage, Bob and I would have it all together. Everything figured out. Everything wired. Everything humming along like a well-oiled machine. That's a nice thought, but marriage is not a machine. It's a human relationship, and every relationship needs work, care, and attention—and sometimes suffers from neglect and withers a bit through indifference.

To this day Bob and I put daily thought, effort, and prayer into our relationship. Are there still speed bumps along our marriage highway? Of course there are. And those are times when we need to humble ourselves before God and each other to make things right. And Bob and I not only live together as husband and wife, but we also work together. Many women tell me it would be a disaster working with their husbands—that it would be way too stressful and frustrating. Yet Bob and I have worked together since 1982, and though we'll never be perfect, we've established a way of working in harmony and love working toward goals we value and desire.

Bob's strengths compensate for my weaknesses, and my strengths compensate for his weaknesses. We balance one another and help each other in those areas where each of us needs the most help. Isn't that what Solomon was talking about in the book of Ecclesiastes? Bob and I understand one another's temperaments, we know each other's quirks, and we're aware of each other's uniqueness.

My friend Donna Otto is a lovely, godly woman and author. Her acrostic helps us remember how to demonstrate respect for our husband. R-A-V-E over him:

> R—respect him with deeds and words
>
> A—allow him to lead spiritually
>
> V—value him above others
>
> E—encourage him in little and big ways

Here is my most important message for this devotion: Let your man know you need him.

"Well, Emilie," you say, "I think he already knows that."

Are you sure? It's like that old cliché about the man who never says "I love you" to his wife. "Why should I?" he grouses. "I told her I loved her on our wedding day 49 years ago, and if that ever changes, I'll let her know." That wouldn't cut it with you, would it? Why? Because you want to hear those crucial words. You want him to look you in the eyes and speak those words to you from his heart as often as possible. And when he does, it fulfills something deep inside you.

When my Bob tells me he loves me, it feels like everything is right in my world—no matter what else is going on. Admittedly I've had to work with him on this communication through the years. I've told him, "Honey, if you tell me you love me every day, I'll be a happy woman the rest of my life."

And it's really no different for a man. He also needs to hear you say "I love you." And he also needs to hear you admit you need him. Being needed is a vital part of a man's makeup.

There is a time when we must firmly choose the course we
must follow, or the relentless drift of events will make the
decision for us.

—HERBERT V. PROCHNOW

Prayer: Father God, let me take nothing for granted in
my relationship with my husband. I want to be
an encourager at all times. Amen.

Action: Be there for your husband when he falls and needs
help in getting up.

Fear of the Lord

The fear of the LORD is the beginning of wisdom;
all who follow his precepts have good understanding.
To him belongs eternal praise.

PSALM 111:10

The motto of the wisdom teachers is that the fear of the Lord (showing holy respect and reverence for God and shunning evil) is the starting point and essence of wisdom. When one has a fear of the Lord they express that respect by having submission to His will.

- "Behold, the fear of the LORD, that is wisdom; and to depart from evil is understanding" (Job 28:28 NASB).

- "The fear of the LORD is the beginning of wisdom, and the knowledge of the Holy One is understanding" (Proverbs 9:10 NASB).

- "The fear of the LORD is the instruction for wisdom, and before honor comes humility" (Proverbs 15:33).

It is also the starting point and essence of wisdom. Wisdom is not acquired by a mechanical formula, but through a right relationship with God. It seems that following God's principles and commandments should be the obvious conclusion of our thankfulness for all He has done for us.

In today's church world, many people have lost the concept of fearing God. The soft side of Christianity has preached only the "love of God." We haven't balanced the scale by teaching the other side of justice and judgment—fear, anger, wrath, obedience, and punishment. Just because some pastors don't teach it from their pulpits doesn't make it less a reality. As with involvement with drugs, alcohol, lust, and envy, we must respect the consequences of our actions or we will be destroyed by their side effects. Our benchmark on all these life destroyers is to have a proper respect for God—He isn't a big daddy upstairs who never asks us to do anything we don't want to do. We must understand that there are consequences for those behaviors we adopt that go against God's will. The good news is that when we are obedient to His precepts, it helps us to stay away from temptation. When we respect God we commit our thoughts to Him, and we choose to give over our lives to Him and His purposes for us.

God lights the way for our paths; we must be willing to follow His lighted path.

Prayer: Father God, fill me with an awesome respect for You. I want to be obedient to Your mighty precepts. Amen.

Action: Exhibit a new respect for your all-powerful God.

Why Are We So Different?

You formed my inward parts;
You wove me in my mother's womb.

PSALM 139:13

I don't understand why my husband can't be like me. I think one way and he seems always to go in the opposite direction. He knows I'm always right (most of the time), but we spend so much time arguing about our differences.

If you have been married for any length of time, you realize that your mate is certainly different from yourself. You may often ask, "Why can't he be like me?" The saying around our home is "Men are weird and wives are strange."

That is so very true—and God designed us that way! We are in a real sense "prescription babies" in that God has a custom design for each of us, equipping us for specific purposes and achievements. The Lord has woven and knitted together our beings in the wombs of our mothers.

Men and women are dissimilar in many ways, including physiology, anatomy, thought patterns, cultural roles, height, weight, strength, compassion, and emotional expression. For the most part, these differences are the result of God's design. Genesis 1:27 reads:

God created man in his own image, in the image of God
he created him; male and female he created them.

And God called His creation good. We get a glimpse of God's
marvelous plan in human creation. Men and women, though different,
are made in God's image.

You can move into your marriage relationship with the confidence
that God has put each partner on the earth for a special purpose. As
loving mates, our task is to investigate to see what that purpose is and
then do all we can to encourage and assist our mates so that they can
become all that God has planned for them.

We have a choice: We can live in war zones fueled by conflict
and frustration, or we can live in homes filled with the precious and
pleasant riches that come from understanding and accepting our difference. Difference brings variation, and variation brings challenges
and interest! Cherish your differences!

> Raised voices lower esteem. Hot tempers cool friendships.
> Loose tongues stretch truth. Swelled heads shrink influence.
> Sharp words dull respect.
>
> —WILLIAM A. WARD

Prayer: Father God, I want to break down my wall of pride
so I can enjoy all the differences between me and
my husband. You have created us to be different.
Amen.

Action: Begin to embrace your differences. Talk about them,
and stop trying to change your husband.

Too Much to Do

We hear that some among you are leading
an undisciplined life, doing no work
at all, but acting like busybodies.

2 THESSALONIANS 3:11 NASB

Too many things on your "to-do" list today? Are you overwhelmed with children, house, husband, laundry, meal preparation, work, marketing, and all the multitude of things it takes to run your life?

Has your pursuit of the daily routine left you with no prayer time, no time for Bible study, or no time for even just a few moments of quiet reflection? I know what it's like when that which your heart craves—fellowship with God—just doesn't seem to fit in the schedule. And yet the busier we are, the more we need to be spiritually fit to meet the day's demands.

As a young mom with five children under five, it was difficult for me to put God first, but when I did, my days went so much better. I was able to have a peaceful heart and a sweeter spirit, and it was much more likely that the priorities of my day fell into place after even a brief time with the Lord. My day was brightened when I took time to praise God for my family and for His love.

Because your love is better than life, my lips will glorify you.
I will praise you as long as I live, and in your name I will lift
up my hands. My soul will be satisfied as with the richest
of foods; with singing lips my mouth will praise you.

PSALM 63:3-5

Today with grown children and five grandchildren, I can see even
more clearly what's really important in life. It's that quiet time when I
get to know God's Word, pray God's Word, and walk in God's Word
and His promises.

Don't make the mistake of getting so busy you don't have time
for God. The less time you spend in God's Word, the more time you
spend on yourself.

Prayer: Father God, make me aware of the important issues
of life. Make my desire to be with You a reality. I
truly want to be a mom and grandmom for God.
Amen.

Action: Make a "to-do" list that has spending time with
God at the top of the list.

How Much for a Whistle?

Esau...sold his own birthright for a single meal.
HEBREWS 12:16 NASB

Have you ever laughed at someone who paid a ridiculous price for a dress, gown, or a piece of furniture? I sometimes look in the latest fashion magazine and see that a certain purse might cost $750 dollars. I say to myself, "Who in her right mind would pay that much for a simple purse?"

One of our great Americans, Ben Franklin, tells a little story about a whistle. It brings home the common sense of not selling one's birthright. You've often heard that common sense is not so common anymore— and how true that is.

When Ben was only seven years old, he was charmed by the whistle of a friend and impetuously traded all the pennies he had to his friend for this noisemaker. His purchase made him the target of his family and friends, who pointed out to him the folly of bargaining before reflecting on the worth of one's purchase.

In our lives we run across a lot of whistles for sale. Our common-sense question is, "Are we paying too much for the whistle?" This is especially true when it comes to trading our reputation for a trinket. A woman has a husband who travels a lot and she has become bored with her lifestyle. A very nice gentleman friend helped her break up her boredom by taking her out to dinner and to the theater. What had been a casual occasion has now become a regular occurrence. Is she paying too much for the whistle?

What is a whistle worth? As Christian women we must use the Word of God to help us determine the value of the whistles in our lives. Many times we must answer, "That whistle isn't worth the asking price."

Prayer: Father God, when we find ourselves looking to the future because we aren't content with today, may You give us a peace of mind that lets us rest where You have placed us. Amen.

Action: Tell the story of Ben Franklin's whistle to your children at dinner tonight. After you share a time when you paid too much for a whistle, ask them if they can think of a time when they have done the same.

Always Means Always

[Love] always protects, always trusts,
always hopes, always perseveres.
1 CORINTHIANS 13:7

Sometimes it's hard for us mere mortals to understand adequately the word "always." In today's culture we don't understand love as that kind of commitment. When we say "always," don't we usually mean "sometimes"...or "most of the time"? But "always " really means eternal and everlasting. Can we really commit to always?

When God through Scripture says "always," it means "always"—no exception. Never changing and dependable for eternity. I am challenged when Paul says that love always does these things:

1. protects
2. trusts
3. hopes
4. perseveres

I so want my husband and children to honor me with that kind of love. I want to be a woman who is known for her word: "When Mom says something, you can take it to the bank." In this regard, my advice to moms is, "Just do what you say you are going to do." By so doing, you teach your children the meaning of being trustworthy. You also teach them to trust others—and that's a rare quality in this age of cynicism. But I've learned that he or she who trusts others will make fewer mistakes than the person who distrusts others.

The Living Bible translates Romans 8:24 as follows: "We are saved by trusting. And trusting means looking forward to getting something we don't yet have—for a man who already has something doesn't need to hope and trust that he will get it."

We are to be people of integrity. Our word can always be trusted. When we are these kind of women, our husbands, our children, and our friends will stand at the gate and call us blessed.

Prayer: Almighty, I want to be an "always" person. When I say something, I want it always to be true. My friends can say, "If she said it, it must be true." What a great responsibility to be that kind of woman. Amen.

Action: Which of God's promises do you depend on most? Share these with your family and make the same promises to them. Let them have a chance to make promises too. In love, remind one another of these godly covenants from time to time. Give thanks for God's commitment to all of His promises.

Notes

1. Emilie Barnes, Kay Arthur, and Donna Otto, adapted from *Youniquely Woman* (Eugene, OR: Harvest House Publishers, 2008), pp. 54-55.

2. Emilie Barnes, adapted from *The Heart of Loveliness* (Eugene, OR: Harvest House Publishers, 2001), pp. 22-23.

3. Emilie Barnes, Kay Arthur, and Donna Otto, adapted from *Youniquely Woman,* pp. 171-72.

4. Charles R. Swindoll, *Growing Strong in the Seasons of Life* (Portland, OR: Multnomah Press, 1983), p. 83.

5. Emilie Barnes, Kay Arthur, and Donna Otto, adapted from *Youniquely Woman,* pp. 101-03.

6. Bob Barnes, adapted from *Men Under Construction* (Eugene, OR: Harvest House Publishers, 2006), pp. 166-68.

For more information regarding speaking engagements and additional material, please send a self-addressed envelope to:

More Hours in My Day
2150 Whitestone Dr.
Riverside, CA 92506

Or you can visit us on the Internet at:
www.emiliebarnes.com
or
emilie@emiliebarnes.com

Other Books by Emilie Barnes

15 Minutes Alone with God

15 Minutes Alone with God is designed to help women develop consistent devotional habits. At the same time it does more than teach women how to organize their quiet times. It's also filled with warm, open meditations Emilie has written especially for busy women, providing encouragement and direction for the day from someone who's been there.

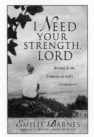

I Need Your Strength, Lord

When home-management expert and best-selling author Emilie Barnes opened her heart in the devotionals *Fill My Cup, Lord* (more than 113,000 copies sold) and *Help Me Trust You, Lord,* readers responded to her message of experiencing God's healing touch in her life.

Now Emilie writes about the health challenges she has faced in recent years, broken family relationships and the process of healing, and God's unfailing peace and loving presence in the midst of darkness. As women lift their prayers to the Lord and ask Him to fill them with hope, they will grow in their walk with Him like never before and be able to offer the gift of encouragement to someone who needs it just as much as they do.

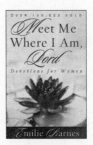

Meet Me Where I Am, Lord

In these short meditations created especially for busy women, best-selling author Emilie Barnes offers prayers, devotions, and Scriptures to lead women to God's presence for lasting refreshment and inspiration.

To learn more about books by Emilie Barnes
or to read sample chapters, log on to our website:

www.harvesthousepublishers.com

HARVEST HOUSE PUBLISHERS

EUGENE, OREGON